THE PSYCHOPATH TEST

ALSO BY JON RONSON

THE PSYCHOPATH TEST

JON RONSON

A Journey Through the Madness Industry

PICADOR

First published 2011 by Picador

First published in paperback 2011 by Picador

This edition first published 2012 by Picador
an imprint of Pan Macmillan
20 New Wharf Road, London N1 9RR
Associated companies throughout the world
www.panmacmillan.com

ISBN 978-0-330-49227-0

33

A CIP catalogue record for this book is available from
the British Library.

Printed and bound by CPI Group (UK) Ltd, Croydon, CR0 4YY

For Anita Bhoomkar (1966–2009)

A lover of life and all its madness.

CONTENTS

1

THE MISSING PART OF THE PUZZLE REVEALED

This is a story about madness. It begins with a curious encounter at a Costa Coffee shop in Bloomsbury, Central London. It was the Costa where the neurologists tended to go, the University College London School of Neurology being just around the corner. And here was one now, turning onto Southampton Row, waving a little self-consciously at me. Her name was Deborah Talmi. She looked like someone who spent her days in laboratories and wasn't used to peculiar rendezvous with journalists in cafes and finding herself at the heart of baffling mysteries. She had brought someone with her. He was a tall, unshaven, academic-looking young man. They sat down.

'I'm Deborah,' she said.

'I'm Jon,' I said.

'I'm James,' he said.

'So,' I asked. 'Did you bring it?'

Deborah nodded. She silently slid a package across the table. I opened it and turned it over in my hands.

'It's quite beautiful,' I said.

Last July, Deborah received a strange package in the mail. It was waiting for her in her pigeonhole. It was postmarked *Gothenburg, Sweden*. Someone had written on the padded envelope *Will tell you more when I return!* But whoever had sent it didn't leave their name.

The package contained a book. It was only forty-two pages long, twenty-one of which – every other page – were completely blank, but everything about it, the paper, the illustrations, the typeface, looked very expensively produced. The cover was a delicate, eerie picture of two disembodied hands drawing each other. Deborah recognized it as a reproduction of M. C. Escher's *Drawing Hands*.

The author was a 'Joe K' (a reference to Kafka's Joseph K, maybe, or an anagram of 'joke'?) and the title was *Being or Nothingness*, which was some kind of allusion to Sartre's 1943 essay, *Being and Nothingness*. Someone had carefully cut out with scissors the page that would have listed the publishing and copyright details, the ISBN number, etc., so there were no clues there. A sticker read, '*Warning! Please study the letter to Professor Hofstadter before you read the book. Good Luck!*'

Deborah leafed through it. It was obviously some kind of a puzzle waiting to be solved, with cryptic verse and pages where words had been cut out, and so on. She looked again at the *Will tell you more when I return!* One of her colleagues was visiting Sweden, and so even though he wasn't normally the sort of person to send out mysterious packages, the most logical explanation was that it had come from him.

But then he returned, and she asked him, and he said he didn't know anything about it.

Deborah was intrigued. She went on the Internet. And it was then she discovered she wasn't alone.

'Were the recipients all neurologists?' I asked her.

'No,' she said. 'Many were neurologists. But one was an astrophysicist from Tibet. Another was a religious scholar from Iran.'

'They were all academics,' said James.

They had all received the package the exact same way Deborah had – in a padded envelope from Gothenburg upon which was written *Will tell you more when I return!* They had gathered on blogs and message-boards and were trying to crack the code.

Maybe, suggested one recipient, the book should be read as a Christian allegory, 'even from the enigmatic *Will tell you more when I return!* (Clearly a reference to the Second Coming of Jesus.) The author/authors seem to be contradicting Sartre's atheist "Being AND Nothingness" (not B OR N).'

A researcher in perceptual psychology called Sarah Allred agreed: 'I have a vague suspicion this is going to end up being some viral marketing / advertising ploy by some sort of religious organization in which academics / intellectuals / scientists / philosophers will come off looking foolish.'

To others this seemed unlikely: 'The expensiveness factor rules out the viral theory unless the campaign is counting on their carefully-selected targets to ponder about the mysterious book online.'

Most of the recipients believed the answer lay, intriguingly, with them. *They* had been hand-picked to receive the package. There was clearly a pattern at work, but what was it? Had they all attended the same conference together years ago or something? Maybe they were being headhunted for a top position in some secretive business?

'First one to crack the code gets the job so to speak?' wrote one Australian recipient.

What seemed obvious was that a brilliant person or organization with ties to Gothenburg had devised a puzzle so complex that even clever academics like them couldn't decipher it. Perhaps it couldn't be decoded because the code was incomplete. Maybe there was a missing piece. Someone suggested 'holding the letter closely over a lamp or try the iodine vapor test on it. There may be some secret writing on it in another type of ink.'

But there didn't turn out to be any secret writing.

They threw up their hands in defeat. If this was a puzzle that academics couldn't solve, maybe they should bring in someone more brutish, like a private investigator or a journalist. Deborah asked around. Which reporter might be tenacious and intrigued enough to engage with the mystery?

They went through a few names.

And then Deborah's friend James said, 'What about Jon Ronson?'

On the day I received Deborah's email inviting me to the Costa Coffee I was in the midst of quite a bad anxiety attack. I had been interviewing a man named Dave McKay. He was the charismatic leader of a small Australian religious group called the Jesus Christians and had recently suggested to his members that they each donate their spare kidney to a stranger. Dave and I had got on pretty well at first – he'd seemed engagingly eccentric and I was consequently gathering good material for my story, enjoyably nutty quotes from him, etc. – but when I proposed that group pressure, emanating from Dave, was perhaps the reason why some of his more vulnerable members might be choosing to give up a kidney, he exploded. He sent me a message saying that to teach me a lesson he was putting the brakes on an imminent kidney donation. He would let the recipient die and her death would be on my conscience.

I was horrified for the recipient and also quite pleased that Dave had sent me such a mad message that would be good for my story. I told a journalist that he seemed quite psychopathic (I didn't know a thing about psychopaths but I assumed that that was the sort of thing they might do). The journalist printed the quote. A few days later Dave emailed me: 'I consider it defamatory to state that I am a psychopath. I have sought legal advice. I have been told that I have a strong case against you. Your malice toward me does not allow you to defame me.'

This was what I was massively panicking about on the day Deborah's email to me arrived in my inbox.

'What was I *thinking*?' I said to my wife, Elaine. 'I was just enjoying being interviewed. I was just enjoying talking. And now it's all fucked. Dave McKay is going to sue me.'

'What's happening?' yelled my son, Joel, entering the room. 'Why is everyone shouting?'

'I made a silly mistake, I called a man a psychopath, and now he's angry,' I explained.

'What's he going to do to us?' said Joel.

There was a short silence.

'Nothing,' I said.

'But if he's not going to do anything to us why are you worried?' said Joel.

'I'm just worried that I've made him angry,' I said. 'I don't like to make people upset or angry. That's why I'm sad.'

'You're lying,' said Joel, narrowing his eyes. 'I *know* you don't mind making people angry or upset. What is it that you aren't telling me?'

'I've told you everything,' I said.

'Is he going to attack us?' said Joel.

'No!' I said. 'No, no! That definitely won't happen!'

'Are we in danger?' yelled Joel.

'He's not going to attack us,' I yelled. 'He's just going to sue us. He just wants to take away my money.'

'Oh God,' said Joel.

I sent Dave an email apologizing for calling him psychopathic.

'Thank you, Jon,' he replied right away. 'My respect for you has risen considerably. Hopefully if we should ever meet again we can do so as something a little closer to what might be called friends.'

'And so,' I thought, 'there was me once again worrying about nothing.'

I checked my unread emails and found the one from Deborah Talmi. She said she and many other academics around the world had received a mysterious package in the mail. She'd heard from a friend who had read my books that I was the sort of journalist who might enjoy odd whodunits. She ended with, 'I hope I've conveyed to you the sense of weirdness that I feel about the whole thing, and how alluring this story is. It's like an adventure story, or an alternative reality game, and we're all pawns in it. By sending it to researchers, they have invoked the researcher in me, but I've failed to find the answer. I hope very much that you'll take it up.'

Now, in the Costa Coffee, she glanced over at the book, which I was turning over in my hands.

'In essence,' she said, 'someone is trying to capture specific academics' attention to something in a very mysterious way and I'm curious to know why. I think it's too much of an elaborate campaign for it to be just a private individual. The book is trying to tell us something. But I don't know what. I would love to know who sent it to me, and why, but I have no investigative talents.'

'Well . . .' I said.

I fell silent and gravely examined the book. I sipped my coffee.

'I'll give it a try,' I said.

• • •

I told Deborah and James that I'd like to begin my investigation by looking around their workplaces. I said I was keen to see the pigeonhole where Deborah had first discovered the package. They covertly shared a glance to say, 'That's an odd place to start but who dares to second guess the ways of the great detectives.'

Their glance may not, actually, have said that. It might instead have said, 'Jon's investigation could not benefit in any serious way from a tour of our offices and it's slightly strange that he wants to do it. Let's hope we haven't picked the wrong journalist. Let's hope he isn't some kind of a weirdo, or has a private agenda for wanting to see inside our buildings.'

If their glance did say that they would have been correct: I did have a private agenda for wanting to see inside their buildings.

James's department was a crushingly unattractive concrete slab just off Russell Square, the University College London School of Psychology. Fading photographs on the corridor walls from the 1960s and 1970s showed children strapped to frightening-looking machines, wires dangling from their heads. They smiled at the camera in uncomprehending excitement as if they were at the beach.

A stab had clearly once been made at de-uglifying these public spaces by painting a corridor a jaunty yellow. This was because, it turned out, babies come here to have their brains tested and someone thought the yellow might calm them. But I couldn't see how. Such was the oppressive ugliness of this building it would have been

like sticking a red nose on a cadaver and calling it Ronald
McDonald.

I glanced into offices. In each a neurologist or psychologist was hunkered down over their desk, concentrating hard on something brain-related. In one room, I
learnt, the field of interest was a man from Wales who
could recognize all his sheep as individuals but couldn't
recognize human faces, not even his wife, not even himself in the mirror. The condition is called prosopagnosia
– face-blindness. Sufferers are apparently forever inadvertently insulting their workmates and neighbours and
husbands and wives by not smiling back at them when
they pass them on the street, and so on. People can't
help taking offence even if they know the rudeness is the
fault of the disorder and not haughtiness. Bad feelings
can spread.

In another office a neurologist was studying the
July 1996 case of a doctor, a former RAF pilot, who
flew over a field in broad daylight, turned around, flew
back over it fifteen minutes later, and there, suddenly,
was a vast crop circle. It was as if it had just *material-
ized*. It covered ten acres and consisted of a hundred
and fifty-one separate circles. The circle, dubbed the
Julia Set, became the most celebrated in crop-circle history. T-shirts and posters were printed. Conventions
were organized. The movement had been dying off
– it had become increasingly obvious that crop circles
were built not by extra-terrestrials but by conceptual
artists in the dead of night using planks of wood and
string – but this one had appeared from nowhere in the
fifteen-minute gap between the pilot's two journeys over
the field.

The neurologist in this room was trying to work out why the pilot's brain had failed to spot the circle the first time around. It had been there all along, having been built the previous night by a group of conceptual artists known as Team Satan using planks of wood and string.

The Julia Set crop circle.

In a third office I saw a woman with a *Little Miss Brainy* book on her shelf. She seemed cheerful and breezy and good-looking.

'Who's that?' I asked James.

'Essi Viding,' he said.

'What does she study?' I asked.

'Psychopaths,' said James.

I peered in at Essi. She spotted us, smiled and waved.

'That must be dangerous,' I said.

'I heard a story about her once,' said James. 'She was interviewing a psychopath. She showed him a picture of a frightened face and asked him to identify the emotion. He said he didn't know what the emotion was but it was the face people pulled just before he killed them.'

I continued down the corridor. Then I stopped and glanced back at Essi Viding. I'd never really thought much about psychopaths before that moment and I wondered if I should try and meet some. It seemed extraordinary that there were people out there whose neurological condition, according to James's story, made them so terrifying, like a wholly malevolent space creature from a sci-fi movie. I vaguely remembered hearing psychologists say there was a preponderance of psychopaths at the top, in the corporate and political worlds – a clinical absence of empathy being a benefit in those environments. Could that really be true? Essi waved at me again. And I decided, no, it would be a mistake to start meddling in the world of psychopaths, an especially big mistake for someone like me who suffers from a surfeit of anxiety. I waved back and continued down the corridor.

Deborah's building, the University College London Wellcome Trust Centre for Neuroimaging, was just around the corner on Queen Square. It was more modern and equipped with Faraday cages and fMRI scanners operated by geeky-looking technicians wearing comic-book T-shirts. Their nerdy demeanours made the machines seem less intimidating.

'Our goal,' said the Centre's website, 'is to understand how thought and perception arise from brain activity, and how such processes break down in neuro-logical and psychiatric disease.'

We reached Deborah's pigeonhole. I scrutinized it.

'OK,' I said. 'Right.'

I stood nodding for a moment. Deborah nodded back. We looked at each other.

Now was surely the time to reveal to her my secret agenda for wanting to get inside their buildings. It was that my anxiety levels had gone through the roof those past months. It wasn't normal. Normal people definitely didn't feel this panicky. Normal people definitely didn't feel like they were being electrocuted from the inside by an unborn child armed with a miniature taser, that they were being prodded by a wire emitting the kind of electrical charge that stops cattle from going into the next field. And so my plan all day, ever since the Costa Coffee, had been to steer the conversation to the subject of my over-anxious brain and maybe Deborah would offer to put me in an fMRI scanner or something. But she'd seemed so delighted that I'd agreed to solve the *Being or Nothingness* mystery I hadn't so far had the heart to mention my flaw, lest it spoiled the mystique.

Now was my last chance. Deborah saw me staring at her, poised to say something important.

'Yes?' she said.

There was a short silence. I looked at her.

'I'll let you know how I get on,' I said.

The 6 a.m. discount Ryanair flight to Gothenburg was packed and claustrophobic and cramped. I tried to reach down into my trouser pocket to retrieve my notepad so I could write a to-do list, but my leg was impossibly wedged underneath the tray table that was piled high with the remainder of my snack-pack breakfast. I needed to plan for Gothenburg. I really could have done with my notepad. My memory isn't what it used to be. Quite frequently these days, in fact, I set off from my home with an excited, purposeful expression and after a while I slow to a stop and just stand there looking puzzled. In moments like that everything becomes dreamlike and muddled. My memory will probably go altogether one day, just like my father's has, and there will be no books to write then. I really need to accumulate a nest egg.

I tried to reach down to scratch my foot. I couldn't. It was trapped. It was fucking trapped. It was *fucking* . . .

'YEAL!' I involuntarily yelled. My leg shot upwards, hitting the tray table. The passenger next to me gave me a startled look. I had just let out an *unintentional shriek*. I stared straight ahead, looking shocked but also slightly awed. I didn't realize that such mysterious, crazy noises existed within me.

I had a lead in Gothenburg, the name and business address of a man who might know the identity or identities of 'Joe K'. His name was Petter Nordlund. Although none of the packages sent to the academics contained any leads – no names of possible authors or distributors – somewhere, buried deep within the archive of a Swedish library, I had found 'Petter Nordlund' referenced as the English translator of *Being or Nothingness*.

A Google search revealed nothing more about him, only the address of a Gothenburg company called BIR he was somehow involved in.

If, as the book's recipients suspected, a team of clever puzzle-makers was behind this expensive, enigmatic campaign for reasons not yet established (religious propaganda? Viral marketing? Headhunting?), Petter Nordlund was my only way in. But he didn't know I was coming. I'd been afraid he'd go to ground if he did. Or maybe he'd tip off whichever shadowy organization was behind *Being or Nothingness*. Maybe they'd try to stop me in some way I couldn't quite visualize. Whatever, I determined that doorstepping Petter Nordlund was the shrewdest course of action. It was a gamble. The whole journey was a gamble. Translators often work at a great distance from their clients and Petter Nordlund might well have known nothing at all.

Some recipients had suggested that *Being or Nothingness* was a puzzle that couldn't be decoded because it was incomplete, and after studying the book for a week I'd come to agree. Each page seemed to be a riddle with a solution that was just out of reach.

A note at the beginning claimed that the manuscript had been 'found' in the corner of an abandoned railway station: 'It was lying in the open, visible to all, but I was the only one curious enough to pick it up.'

What followed were elliptical quotations:

My thinking is muscular.
ALBERT EINSTEIN

I am a strange loop.

DOUGLAS HOFSTADTER

Life is meant to be a joyous adventure.

JOE K

The book had only twenty-one pages that weren't blank, but some pages contained just one sentence. Page 18, for instance, simply read: 'The sixth day after I stopped writing the book I sat at B's place and wrote the book.'

And all of this was very expensively produced, using the highest quality paper and inks – there was a full-colour, delicate reproduction of a butterfly on one page – and the endeavour must have cost someone or a group of people an awful lot of money.

The missing piece hadn't turned out to be secret writing in invisible ink but there was another possibility. On page 13 of every copy a hole had been assiduously cut out. Some words were missing. Was the solution to the mystery somehow connected to those missing words?

I picked up a rental car at Gothenburg airport. The smell of it – the smell of a newly cleaned rental car – never fails to bring back happy memories of past sleuthing adventures. There were the weeks I spent trailing the conspiracy theorist David Icke as he hypothesized his theory that the secret rulers of the world were giant blood-drinking child-sacrificing paedophile lizards that had adopted human form. That was a good story. And it began, as this one had, with the smell of a newly cleaned hire car.

The satnav took me past the Liseberg funfair, past the stadium where Madonna was due to play the next night, and on towards the business district. I imagined Petter Nordlund's office would be located there, but instead the satnav told me to take a sharp unexpected left and I found myself bouncing up a tree-lined residential street towards a giant white square clapboard house.

This was, it told me, my destination.

I walked to the front door and rang the buzzer. A woman in jogging pants answered.

'Is this Petter Nordlund's office?' I asked her.

'This is his home,' she said.

'Oh, I'm sorry,' I said. 'Is he here?'

'He's with patients today,' she said. She had an American accent.

'He's a doctor?' I asked.

'A psychiatrist,' she said.

We stood on her doorstep and talked for a while. She said her name was Lily and she was Petter's wife. They'd been childhood sweethearts (he went to school in America) and had been considering settling in her home state of California but then Petter's uncle died and he inherited this huge house and they just couldn't resist.

Petter, Lily said, was not only a translator but a highly successful psychiatrist. (I later read his LinkedIn page, which said he worked with schizophrenics and psychotics and OCD sufferers, and had also been a 'protein chemist' and an adviser to both an 'international investment company' and a 'Cambridge biotech company' specializing in something called 'therapeutic peptide discovery and development'.) He was working in a clinic two hours outside Gothenburg, she said, and, no, there was no point in me driving over there. They would never let me in without the proper accreditation.

'*I* can't even get a hold of him when he's with patients,' she said. 'It's very intense.'

'Intense in what way?' I asked.

'I don't even know that!' she said. 'He'll be back in a few days. If you're still in Gothenburg you're welcome to try again.' She paused. 'So, why are you here? Why do you want to see my husband?'

'He translated a very intriguing book,' I said, 'called *Being or Nothingness*. I've become so fascinated by the book I wanted to meet him and find out who his employer was and why it was written.'

'Oh,' she said. She sounded surprised.

'Do you know *Being or Nothingness*?' I asked her.

'Yeah,' she said. She paused. 'I . . . Yeah. I know which book you're talking about. I . . . He translates several things. For companies. And that was . . .' She trailed off. Then she said, 'We don't get into each other's work. I don't even pay attention to what he's doing, quite honestly! I know he's very much into molecular something, but I don't understand it. Sometimes he says, "I've just translated this for some company," and if it's in Swedish, or something, I don't understand it so I really don't try and look into his work.'

'Anyway, it was lovely talking to you,' I said. 'I'll pop back in a few days?'

'Sure,' said Lily. 'Sure.'

The days that followed passed slowly. I lay in my hotel room and watched the kind of strange European TV that would probably make perfect sense if I understood the language, but because I didn't the programmes just seemed dreamlike and baffling. In one studio show a group of Scandinavian academics watched as one of them poured liquid plastic into a bucket of cold water. It solidified, they pulled it out, handed it around the circle and, as far as I could tell, intellectualized on its random misshapenness. I phoned home but my wife didn't answer. It crossed my mind that she might be dead. I panicked. Then it turned out that she wasn't dead. She had just been at the shops. I have panicked unnecessarily in all four corners of the globe. I took a walk. When I returned there was a message waiting for me. It was from Deborah Talmi. A suspect had emerged. Could I call her?

The suspect, I discovered to my annoyance, wasn't in Sweden. He was in Bloomington, Indiana. His name was Levi Shand and he had just gone online to post the most implausible story about his involvement in *Being or Nothingness*.

Levi Shand's story, Deborah told me, went something like this. He was a student at Indiana University. He'd been driving aimlessly around town when he happened to notice a large brown box sitting in the dirt underneath a railway bridge. So he pulled over to have a closer look at it.

The box was unmarked and noticeably clean, as if it had only recently been dumped there. Even though Levi was nervous about opening it – anything could be in there, from a million dollars to a severed head – he plucked up the courage, and discovered eight pristine copies of *Being or Nothingness*.

He read the stickers on each: '*Warning! Please study the letter to Professor Hofstadter before you read the book. Good Luck!*' and was intrigued. Because he knew who Professor Hofstadter was, and where he lived.

'I'm not familiar with Professor Hofstadter,' I said to Deborah. 'I know there are references to him scattered all over *Being or Nothingness*. But I couldn't work out if he's a real person or a fictional character. Is he well known?'

'He wrote *Gödel, Escher, Bach*!' she replied, surprised by my lack of knowledge. 'It was momentous.'

I didn't reply.

'If you're a geek,' sighed Deborah, 'and you're just discovering the Internet and especially if you're a boy, *Gödel, Escher, Bach* would be like your Bible. It was about how you can use Gödel's mathematic theories and Bach's canons to make sense of the experience of consciousness. Lots of young guys really like it. It's very playful. I haven't read it in its entirety but it's on my bookshelf.'

Hofstadter, she said, had published it in the late 1970s. It was lauded. It won a Pulitzer. It was filled with brilliant puzzles and word play and meditations on the meaning of consciousness and artificial intelligence. It was the kind of book – like *Zen and the Art of Motorcycle Maintenance* or *A Brief History of Time* – that everybody wanted on their shelves but few were clever enough to really understand.

Even though the world had been at Hofstadter's feet in 1979 he had retreated from it, and had instead spent the past three decades working quietly as a professor of cognitive science at Indiana University. But he was well known amongst the students. He had a shock of grey hair like Andy Warhol's and a huge house on the edge of campus, which was where – Levi Shand's story continued – the young student drove with the intention of presenting Hofstadter with the eight copies of *Being or Nothingness* he had found in the box underneath the railway bridge.

'A railway bridge,' I said to Deborah. 'Have you noticed the parallel? In that covering letter to Douglas Hofstadter, the writer talks about finding some old typewritten pages carelessly thrown in the corner of an abandoned railroad station. And now Levi Shand has found some copies of *Being or Nothingness* thrown underneath a railway bridge.'

'You're right!' said Deborah.

'So what does Levi Shand say happened when he went to Hofstadter's house to deliver the books?' I asked.

'He says he knocked on Hofstadter's door and it swung open to reveal to his astonishment a harem of beautiful French women. And standing in the midst of the harem was Hofstadter himself. He invited the open-mouthed young student inside, took the books, thanked him, and showed him to the door again.'

And that, Deborah said, was the end of Levi Shand's story.

We fell into a puzzled silence.

'A harem of beautiful French women?' I said.

'I don't believe the story,' she said.

'It doesn't seem plausible,' I said. 'I wonder if I can get Levi Shand on the phone?'

'I've done some research on him,' Deborah said. 'He's got a Facebook page.'

'Oh, OK,' I said. 'I'll contact him through that, then.'

There was a silence.

'Deborah?' I said.

'I don't think he exists,' Deborah said suddenly.

'But he's got a Facebook page,' I said.

'With three hundred American friends who look the part,' Deborah said.

'You think . . . ?' I said.

'I think someone has created a convincing Facebook persona for Levi Shand,' Deborah said.

I took this possibility in.

'Have you thought about his name?' Deborah asked.

'Levi Shand?'

'Haven't you worked it out?' she said. 'It's an anagram.'

I fell silent.

' "Lavish End"!' I suddenly exclaimed.

'No,' said Deborah.

I got out a piece of paper.

'Devil Has N . . . ? I asked after a while.

' "Live Hands",' said Deborah. 'It's an anagram of "Live Hands".'

'Oh, OK,' I said.

'Like the drawing on the cover of *Being or Nothingness*,' prompted Deborah. 'Two hands drawing each other . . . ?'

'So if Levi Shand doesn't exist,' I said, 'who created him?'

'I think they're all Hofstadter,' said Deborah. 'Levi Shand. Petter Nordlund. I think they're *all Douglas Hofstadter*.'

I went for a walk through Gothenburg, feeling quite annoyed and disappointed that I'd been hanging around here for days when the culprit was probably an eminent professor some four thousand miles away at Indiana University. Deborah had offered me supplementary circumstantial evidence to back her theory that the whole puzzle was a product of Douglas Hofstadter's impish mind. It was, she said, exactly the sort of playful thing he might do. And, being the author of an international bestseller, he would have the financial resources to pull it off. Plus he was no stranger to Sweden. According to his Wikipedia page he lived there in the mid-1960s. Furthermore, *Being or Nothingness* looked like a Hofstadter book. The clean white cover was reminiscent of the cover of Hofstadter's follow-up to *Gödel, Escher, Bach* – 2007's *I Am A Strange Loop*.

True, the creation of a fake Indiana University student with a fake Facebook page and an unlikely tale about a harem of beautiful French women was an odd addition, but it would do no good to second-guess the motives of a brilliant man like Hofstadter.

Furthermore, Deborah believed she had solved the puzzle. Yes, there was a missing piece, but it didn't take the form of invisible ink or significant words cut out of page 13. It was, she said, the way the book had revealed an inherent narcissism in its recipients.

'That's what *I Am A Strange Loop* is about,' said Deborah. 'It's about how we spend our lives self-referencing, over and over, in a kind of strange loop. Now lots of people are asking themselves, "Why was I selected to receive this book?" They aren't talking about the *book* or the *message*. They're talking about *themselves*. So *Being or Nothingness* has created a strange loop of people and it is a vessel for them to self-reference.' She paused. 'I think that's Hofstadter's message.'

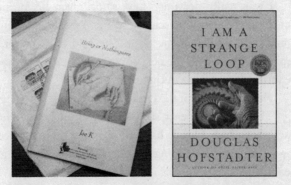

Being or Nothingness, and the package it came in. The American paperback cover of *I Am A Strange Loop*.

It was a compelling theory, and I continued to believe this might be the solution to the riddle right up until the moment, an hour later, I had a Skype video conversation with Levi Shand who, it quickly transpired, wasn't an invention of Douglas Hofstadter but an actual student from Indiana University.

He was a handsome young man with black hair, doleful eyes, and a messy student bedroom. He had been easy to track down. I emailed him via his Facebook page. He got back to me straight away (he'd been online at the time) and within seconds we were face to face.

He told me it was all true. He really did find the books in a box under a railway viaduct and Douglas Hofstadter really did have a harem of French women living at his home.

'Tell me exactly what happened when you visited him,' I said.

'I was really nervous,' Levi said, 'given his prominence on the cognitive-science scene. A beautiful young French girl answered the door. She told me to wait. I looked through into the next room, and there were more beautiful French girls in there.'

'How many in total?' I asked.

'There were at least six of them,' said Levi. 'They had brown hair, blonde hair, all standing there between the kitchen and the dining room. All of them stunningly beautiful.'

'Is this *true*?' I asked him.

'Well, they might have been Belgian,' said Levi.

'What happened then?' I asked.

'Professor Hofstadter came out from the kitchen,' he said, 'looking thin but healthy. Charismatic. He took the books, thanked me, and I left. And that's it.'

'And every word of this is true?' I asked.

'Every word,' said Levi.

• • •

But something didn't feel right. Levi's story, and indeed Deborah's theory, only worked if Douglas Hofstadter was some kind of playful, dilettantish prankster, and nothing I could find suggested he was. In 2007, for example, Deborah Solomon of the *New York Times* asked him some slightly facetious questions and his replies revealed him to be a serious, quite impatient, man:

Q. You first became known in 1979, when you published 'Gödel, Escher, Bach,' a campus classic, which finds parallels between the brains of Bach, M. C. Escher and the mathematician Kurt Gödel. In your new book, 'I Am a Strange Loop,' you seem mainly interested in your own brain.

A. This book is much straighter. It's less crazy. Less daring, maybe.

Q. You really know how to plug a book.

A. Well, O.K., I don't know. Questions of consciousness and soul – that is what the new book was motivated by.

Q. Your entry in Wikipedia says that your work has inspired many students to begin careers in computing and artificial intelligence.

A. I have no interest in computers. The entry is filled with inaccuracies, and it kind of depresses me.

And so on. Hofstadter's work, I learnt, was informed by two neurological tragedies. When he was twelve it became clear that his young sister Molly was unable to speak or understand language: 'I was very interested already in how things in my mind worked,' he told *Time* magazine in 2007. 'When Molly's unfortunate plight became apparent, it all started getting connected to the physical world. It really made you think about the brain and the self, and how the brain determines who the person is.'

And then in 1993 his wife, Carol, died, suddenly, of a brain tumour. Their children were two and five. He was left overwhelmed with grief. In *I Am A Strange Loop* he consoles himself with the thought that she lived on in his brain: 'I believe that there is a trace of her "I", her interiority, her inner light, however you want to phrase it, that remains inside me,' he told *Scientific American* in 2007, 'and the trace that remains is a valid trace of her self—her soul, if you wish. I have to emphasize that the sad truth of the matter is, of course, that whatever persists in me is a very feeble copy of her. It's reduced, a sort of low-resolution version, coarse-grained . . . Of course it doesn't remove the sting of death. It doesn't say, "Oh, well, it didn't matter that she died because she lives on just fine in my brain." Would that it were. But, anyway, it is a bit of a consolation.'

None of this painted a picture of a man who might have a harem of French women and a propensity to create a complicated, odd conspiracy involving posting dozens of strange books, anonymously, to academics across the world.

I wrote him an email, asking him if Levi Shand's story about the box under the bridge and the harem of French women was true, and then I went for a walk. When I returned, this was waiting for me in my inbox:

Dear Mr. Ronson,
I have nothing to do with *Being or Nothingness*

except that I'm mentioned in it. I am just an 'innocent victim' of the project.

Yes, Mr. Shand came to my house and delivered a few copies of the odd book, but the rest of his story is sheer fabrication. My daughter was having her French lesson with her French tutor in the living room, so perhaps Mr. Shand espied the two of them and heard them speaking French. Also, I speak Italian at home with my kids, and for all I know, Mr. Shand may have mistaken the sound of Italian for French. The point is, there was certainly no 'house filled with beautiful French women' – that's utter rubbish. He wanted to make his mission sound mysterious and titillating. It's a shame that people do this kind of thing and post it on the Web.

Sincerely, Douglas Hofstadter

I emailed Hofstadter back. Much of Levi Shand's tale didn't ring true, I said, not only the business of the harem but also the story of how he found the box underneath the railway viaduct. Could it be possible that Levi Shand was in fact the author of *Being or Nothingness*? He replied:

Levi Shand is certainly not the author of the small white book. I have been sent about 80 copies (70 in English, 10 in Swedish) by its author. They sit untouched in my office. Before the book existed, I received a series of extremely cryptic postcards, all in Swedish (all of which I read, although not carefully, and none of which made the least sense at all). People who are normal (i.e., sane, sensible) don't try to open lines of communication with total strangers by writing them a series of disjointed, weird, cryptic messages.

From there on, it only got weirder—first several copies of the book were sent to me in a package, and then, some months later, about 80 copies arrived at my office, and then came the bizarre claim that a bunch of copies "were found under a bridge" on my campus, and then books started arriving at various universities around the world, sent to people in certain disciplines that were vaguely associated with AI, biology, etc. And then there were the scissored-out words (super-weird!), and the taped-in letter, addressed to me. All of it was completely nuts. I could say much more about it all, but I don't have the time.

I have a great deal of experience with people who are smart but unbalanced, people who think they have found the key to the universe, etc. This particular case was exceedingly transparent because it was so exceedingly obsessive.

Yes, there was a missing piece of the puzzle, Douglas Hofstadter was saying, but the recipients had got it wrong. They assumed the endeavour was brilliant and rational because they were brilliant and rational and we tend to automatically assume that everybody else is basically just like us. But in fact the missing piece was that the author was a crackpot. The book couldn't be decoded because it was written by a crackpot.

'Petter Nordlund?' I thought.

Was Petter Nordlund the sole perpetrator? It seemed unlikely that such a successful man – a distinguished psychiatrist and a protein chemist, whatever that was, and an adviser to a biotech company specializing in therapeutic peptide discovery and development, whatever that was, was actually, in Hofstadter's words, an 'extremely obsessive crackpot'.

But at 7 p.m. that evening I was face to face with him, and it became quickly obvious that he was indeed the culprit. He was tall, in his fifties, with an attractive face, the air of an academic. He wore a tweed jacket. He stood in his doorway with his wife at his side. Immediately, I liked him. He had a big, kind, cryptic, smile on his face, and he was wringing his hands like a man possessed. I frequently wring my hands in much the same way. I couldn't help thinking that – in terms of getting much too obsessed about stupid things that didn't matter – Petter and I were probably peas in a pod.

'I'm surprised you're here,' Petter said.

'I hope it isn't too unpleasant a surprise,' I said.

There was a short silence.

'If you study *Being or Nothingness*,' Petter said, 'you will realize that you will never find out the author.'

'I think I know the author,' I said. 'I think it's you.'

'That's easy to . . .' Petter tailed off. 'That's an easy guess,' he said.

'Is it a correct guess?' I asked.

'Of course not,' said Petter.

Petter (and Petter Nordlund is not his real name, nor is Lily her real name) bounced up and down on his feet a little. He was adopting the demeanour of a man who had received an unexpected visit from a neighbour just as something was boiling over on the stove. But I could tell his air of friendly distraction was a mask and underneath he was feeling quite overwhelmed by my arrival.

'Petter,' I said. 'Let me at least ask you this. Why were those particular people chosen to receive the book?'

At this Petter let out a small gasp. His face lit up. It was as if I had just asked him the most wonderful question that could be asked.

'Well . . . !' he said.

'How would you know who got the book?' Lily quickly interrupted, a sharpness in her voice. 'You only translated it.'

And, with that, the moment passed. Petter's face once again took on the mask of polite distraction.

'Yes,' he said. 'Yes. I really am sorry but I'm going to have to end . . . My intention was just to say hi and go back. I have said more than I should . . . You talk to my wife now.'

Petter backed away then, smiling, back into the shadows of his house, and Lily and I looked at each other.

'I'm going to Norway now,' she said. 'Goodbye.'

'Goodbye,' I said.

I flew back to London.

There was an email waiting for me from Petter. 'You seem like a nice man. The first step of the project will be over soon and it will be up to others to take it to the next level. Whether you will play a part I don't know—but you will know . . .'

'I would be glad to play a part if you give me some guidance as to how I might do so,' I wrote back.

'Well you see, that is the tricky part, knowing what to do,' he replied. 'We call it life! Trust me, when your time comes you will know.'

Several weeks passed. My time didn't come, or if it did come I didn't notice. Finally I telephoned Deborah and told her that I had solved the mystery.

I sat outside the Starbucks in the Brunswick Centre, Russell Square, Central London, and watched as Deborah turned the corner and walked fast towards me. She sat down and smiled.

'So?' she said.

'Well . . .' I said.

I recounted to her my conversations with Levi Shand and Douglas Hofstadter, my meetings with Petter and Lily, and my subsequent email correspondence. When I finished she looked at me and she said, 'Is that *it*?'

'Yes!' I said. 'It all happened because the author was – according to Hofstadter – a crackpot. Everyone was looking for the missing piece of the puzzle, and the missing piece turned out to be *that*.'

'Oh,' she said.

She looked disappointed.

'But it *isn't* disappointing,' I said. 'Can't you see? It's incredibly interesting. Aren't you struck by how much *action* occurred simply because something went wrong with one man's brain? It's as if the rational world, your world, was a still pond and Petter's brain was a jagged rock thrown into it, creating odd ripples everywhere.'

The thought of this suddenly excited me hugely: Petter Nordlund's craziness had had a huge influence on the world. It caused intellectual examination, economic activity, and formed a kind of community. Disparate academics, scattered across continents, had become intrigued and paranoid and narcissistic because of it. They'd met on blogs and message boards and had debated for hours, forming conspiracy theories about shadowy Christian organizations, etc. One of them had felt motivated to rendezvous with me in a Costa Coffee. I'd flown to Sweden in an attempt to solve the mystery. And so on.

I thought about my own over-anxious brain, my own sort of madness. Was it a more powerful engine in my life than my rationality? I remembered those psychologists who said psychopaths made the world go around. They meant it: society was, they claimed, an expression of that particular sort of madness.

Suddenly, madness was everywhere, and I was determined to learn about the impact it had on the way society evolves. I've always believed society to be a fundamentally rational thing, but what if it isn't? What if it is built on insanity?

I told Deborah all of this. She frowned.

'That *Being or Nothingness* thing,' she said. 'Are you *sure* it was all because of one crazy Swedish man?'

2

THE MAN WHO
FAKED MADNESS

DSM-IV-TR is an 886-page textbook published by the American Psychiatric Association that sells for $99. It sits on the shelves of psychiatry offices all over the world and lists every known mental disorder. There are currently 374 known mental disorders. I bought the book soon after I returned from my coffee with Deborah and leafed through it, searching for disorders that might compel the sufferer to try and achieve a position of power and influence over others. Surprisingly, this being such a vast book packed with so many disorders, including esoteric ones like Frotteurism ('rubbing against a non-consenting person in a public transportation vehicle while usually fantasizing an exclusive, caring relationship with the victim, most acts of frottage occur when the person is aged 12–15, after which there is a gradual decline in frequency') there was nothing at all in there about psychopaths. Maybe there had been some backstage schism in the psychopath-defining world? The closest I could find was Narcissistic Personality Disorder, sufferers of which have 'a grandiose sense of self-importance and entitlement', are 'preoccupied with fantasies of unlimited success', and are 'exploitative', 'lack empathy' and require 'excessive admiration', and Antisocial Personality Disorder, which compels sufferers to be 'frequently deceitful and manipulative in order to gain personal profit or pleasure (e.g., to obtain money, sex or power)'.

'I could really be on to something,' I thought. 'It really could be that many of our political and business leaders suffer from Antisocial or Narcissistic Personality Disorder and they do the harmful, exploitative things they do because of some mad striving for unlimited success and excessive admiration. Their mental disorders might be what rule our lives. This could be a really big story for me if I can think of a way to somehow prove it.'

I closed the manual.

'I wonder if *I've* got any of the 374 mental disorders?' I thought.

I opened the manual again.

And I instantly diagnosed myself with twelve different ones.

General Anxiety Disorder was a given. But I hadn't realized what a collage of mental disorders my whole life has been, from my inability to grasp sums (Arithmetic Learning Disorder) and the resultant tense homework situations with my mother (Parent–Child Relational Problem) right up to the present day, to that *very day*, in fact, which I had spent much of getting jittery with the coffee (Caffeine Induced Disorder) and avoiding work (Malingering). I suspect it was probably unusual to suffer from both General Anxiety Disorder *and* Malingering, unproductiveness tending to make me feel anxious, but there it was. I had both. Even sleep offered no respite from my mental disorders. There was Nightmare Disorder, which is diagnosed when the sufferer dreams of being 'pursued or declared a failure'. *All* my nightmares involve someone chasing me down the street whilst yelling, 'You're a failure!'

I was much crazier than I had imagined. Or maybe it was a bad idea to read DSM-IV when you're not a trained professional. Or maybe the American Psychiatric Association had a crazy desire to label all life a mental disorder.

I knew from seeing stricken loved ones that many of the disorders listed – depression and schizophrenia and obsessive compulsive disorder and so on – are genuine and overwhelming and devastating. But as *Harpers'* L. J. Davis, reviewing the DSM, once wrote, 'It may very well be that the frotteurist is a helpless victim in the clutches of his obsession, but it's equally possible that he's simply a bored creep looking for a cheap thrill.'

I had no idea what to make of it. I decided that if I was to go on a journey to try and spot mental disorders in high places, I needed a second opinion about the authenticity of the labels.

And so I asked around. Was there any organization out there dedicated to documenting the occasions psychiatrists had become overzealous in their labelling and definitely got it wrong? And that's how I ended up having lunch three days later with Brian Daniels.

• • •

Brian is a Scientologist. He works for the British office of an international network of Scientologists called the CCHR (Citizens' Commission on Human Rights), a crack team determined to prove to the world that psychiatrists are wicked and must be stopped. There are Scientologists like Brian in CCHR offices all over the world spending every day of their lives ferreting out stories aimed at undermining the psychiatric profession and getting individual psychiatrists shamed or struck off. Brian was incredibly biased, of course – Tom Cruise once said in a taped speech to Scientologists, 'We are the authorities on the mind!' – but I wanted to hear about the times psychiatry had really got it wrong and nobody knew these stories better than him.

I had found the idea of meeting with a leading Scientologist quite intimidating. I'd heard about their reputation for tirelessly pursuing people they considered the Church's opponents. Would I accidentally say the wrong thing over lunch and find myself tirelessly pursued? But as it turned out, Brian and I got on well. We shared a mistrust of psychiatry. Admittedly Brian's was deep and abiding and I'd only had mine for a few days – largely the result of my disappointing self-diagnosis from the DSM-IV – but it gave us something to talk about over lunch.

Brian recounted to me his recent successes, his highest profile having occurred just a few weeks earlier when his office had managed to topple the hugely successful daytime UK TV psychiatrist Dr Raj Persaud.

Dr Raj had for a long time been a much-loved household name even though he had sometimes been criticized for stating the obvious in his newspaper columns. As the writer Francis Wheen recounted in the *Guardian* in 1996,

After Hugh Grant was arrested [for soliciting the prostitute Divine Brown in Los Angeles in 1995] Raj Persaud was asked by the Daily Mail to analyse Liz Hurley's comments about the affair. He argued: 'The fact that she is "still bewildered" indicates that her shattered understanding of Hugh has yet to be rebuilt . . . Her statement that she is not in a "fit state to make any decisions about the future" is ominous. It suggests that . . . the future is still an open book.'

A year ago, when the new-born baby Abbie Humphries was snatched from a hospital, the Daily Mail wondered what sort of woman could do such a thing. Luckily, Dr Persaud was on hand to explain that the kidnapper may have had some sort of 'need for a baby'.

And so on. In late 2007, Dr Persaud was at Brian's instigation investigated by the General Medical Council for plagiarism. He had written an article attacking Scientology's war on psychiatry, three hundred words of which appeared to be copied verbatim from an earlier attack on the Church by Stephen Kent, a professor of sociology at the University of Alberta in Canada. It seemed a pretty reckless act, knowing how eagle-eyed the Scientologists were reputed to be. Other incidents of plagiarism subsequently came to light and he was found guilty and suspended from practicing psychiatry for three months.

Humiliatingly for Dr Raj, the scrutinizer of celebrities' personality disorders became the scrutinized.

'Is Persaud a narcissist,' asked the Guardian, 'or a

man so plagued by self-doubt that he doesn't obey the rules of academia because he doesn't think he belongs in it?'

Now he no longer appeared on TV or in the newspapers. Brian seemed quietly pleased with his success.

'I'm interested in the idea,' I said to him, 'that many of our leaders suffer from mental disorders . . .'

Brian raised his eyes slightly at the words 'mental disorders'.

'But first,' I said, 'I wanted to make sure that I can depend upon those people who do the diagnoses. So, do you have anything big on the go at the moment that you believe will prove to me that psychiatrists cannot be trusted?'

There was a silence.

'Yes,' said Brian. 'There's Tony.'

'Who's Tony?' I asked.

'Tony's in Broadmoor,' said Brian.

I looked at Brian.

Broadmoor is Broadmoor Psychiatric Hospital. It was once known as Broadmoor Criminal Lunatic Asylum. It was where they sent Ian Brady, the Moors Murderer, who killed three children and two teenagers in the 1960s, and Peter Sutcliffe, the Yorkshire Ripper, who killed thirteen women in the 1970s, creeping up behind them and hitting them over the head with a hammer, and Kenneth Erskine, the Stockwell Strangler, who murdered seven elderly people in 1986, and Robert Napper, who killed Rachel Nickell on Wimbledon Common in July 1992

– he stabbed her forty-nine times in front of her three-year-old son. Broadmoor is where they send the paedophiles and the serial killers and the child-murderers, the ones who couldn't help themselves.

'What did Tony do?' I asked Brian.

'He's completely sane!' said Brian. 'He faked his way in there! And now he's stuck. Nobody will believe he's sane.'

'What do you mean?' I asked.

'He was arrested years ago for something,' said Brian, 'I think he beat someone up or something, and he decided to fake madness to get out of a prison sentence. He thought he'd end up in some cushy local hospital but instead they sent him to Broadmoor! And now he's stuck! The more he tries to convince psychiatrists he's not crazy the more they take it as evidence that he is. He's not a Scientologist or anything but we're helping him with his tribunals. If you want proof that psychiatrists are nuts and they don't know what they're talking about and they make it up as they go along you should meet Tony. Do you want me to try and get you into Broadmoor?'

Was all this true? Was there really a sane man in Broadmoor? I automatically started thinking about what I'd do if I had to prove I was sane. I'd like to think that just being my normal, essentially sane self would be enough, but I'd probably behave in such an overly polite and helpful and competent manner I'd come across like a mad butler with panic in his eyes. Plus it turns out that when I'm placed in an insane environment I tend to get almost instantly crazier, as evidenced by my recent shrieking of the word 'YEAL!' on board the Ryanair flight to Gothenburg.

Did I want to meet Tony?

'OK,' I said.

The Broadmoor visitors' centre was painted in the calming hues of a municipal leisure complex – all peach and pink and pine. The prints on the wall were mass-produced pastel paintings of French doors opening onto beaches at sunrise. The building was called the Wellness Centre.

I had caught the train here from London. I began to yawn uncontrollably around Kempton Park. This tends to happen to me in the face of stress. Apparently dogs do it too. They yawn when anxious.

Brian picked me up at the station and we drove the short distance to the hospital. We passed through two cordons – 'Do you have a mobile phone?' the guard asked me at the first. 'Recording equipment? A cake with a hacksaw hidden inside it? A ladder?' – and then on through gates cut out of high-security fence after fence after fence.

'I think Tony's the only person in the whole DSPD unit to have been given the privilege of meeting people in the Wellness Centre,' Brian said as we waited.

'What does DSPD stand for?' I asked.

'Dangerous and Severe Personality Disorder,' said Brian.

There was a silence.

'Is Tony in the part of Broadmoor that houses the *most dangerous* people?' I asked.

'Crazy, isn't it?' laughed Brian.

• • •

Patients began drifting in to sit with their loved ones at tables and chairs that had been fixed to the ground. They all looked quite similar to each other, quite docile and sad-eyed.

'They're medicated,' whispered Brian.

They were mostly overweight, wearing loose, comfortable T-shirts and elasticated sweatpants. There probably wasn't much to do in Broadmoor but eat.

I wondered if any of them were famous.

They drank tea and ate chocolate bars from the dispenser with their visitors. Most were young, in their twenties, and their visitors were their parents. Some were older, and their partners and children had come to see them.

'Ah! Here's Tony now!' said Brian.

I looked across the room. A man in his late twenties was walking towards us. He wasn't shuffling like the others had. He was sauntering. His arm was outstretched. He wasn't wearing sweatpants. He was wearing a pinstripe jacket and trousers. He looked like a young businessman trying to make his way in the world, someone who wanted to show everyone that he was very, very sane.

And of course, as I watched him approach our table, I wondered if the pinstripe was a clue that he was sane or a clue that he wasn't.

We shook hands.

'I'm Tony,' he said. He sat down.

'So Brian says you faked your way in here,' I said.

'That's exactly right,' said Tony.

He had the voice of a normal, nice, eager-to-help young man.

'I'd committed GBH [grievous bodily harm],' he said. 'After they arrested me I sat in my cell and I thought, "I'm looking at five to seven years." So I asked the other prisoners what to do. They said, "Easy! Tell them you're mad! They'll put you in a county hospital. You'll have Sky TV and a PlayStation. Nurses will bring you pizzas." But they didn't send me to some cushy hospital. They sent me to bloody BROADMOOR.'

'How long ago was this?' I asked.

'Twelve years ago,' said Tony.

I involuntarily grinned.

Tony grinned back.

Tony said faking madness was the easy part, especially when you're seventeen and you take drugs and watch a lot of scary movies. You don't need to know how authentically crazy people behave. You just plagiarize the character Dennis Hopper played in the movie *Blue Velvet*. That's what Tony did. He told a visiting psychiatrist that he liked sending people love letters straight from his heart and a love letter was a bullet from a gun and if you received a love letter from him you'd go straight to hell.

Plagiarizing a well-known movie was a gamble, he said, but it paid off. Lots more psychiatrists began visiting his cell. He broadened his repertoire to include bits from *Hellraiser*, *A Clockwork Orange* and the David Cronenberg movie *Crash*, in which people derive sexual pleasure from enacting car crashes. Tony told the psychiatrists *he* liked to crash cars into walls for sexual pleasure and also that he wanted to kill women because he thought looking into their eyes as they died would make him feel normal.

'Where did you get that one from?' I asked Tony.

'A biography of Ted Bundy,' Tony replied. 'I found it in the prison library.'

I nodded and thought it probably wasn't a great idea for prison libraries to stock books about Ted Bundy.

Brian sat next to us, chuckling wryly about the gullibility and inexactness of the psychiatric profession.

'They took my word for everything,' Tony said.

Tony said the day he arrived at Broadmoor he took one look at the place and realized he'd made a spectacularly bad decision. He asked to speak urgently to psychiatrists.

'I'm not mentally ill,' he told them.

It is an awful lot harder, Tony told me, to convince people you're sane than it is to convince them you're crazy.

'I thought the best way to seem normal,' he said, 'would be to talk to people normally about normal things like football and what's on TV. That's the obvious thing to do, right? I subscribe to *New Scientist*. I like reading about scientific breakthroughs. One time they had an article about how the US Army was training bumblebees to sniff out explosives. So I said to a nurse, "Did you know that the US Army is training bumblebees to sniff out explosives?" Later, when I read my medical notes, I saw they'd written, "Thinks bees can sniff out explosives." '

'When you decided to wear pinstripe to meet me,' I said, 'did you realize the look could go either way?'

'Yes,' said Tony. 'But I thought I'd take my chances. Plus most of the patients here are disgusting slobs who don't wash or change their clothes for weeks on end and I like to dress well.'

I looked around the Wellness Centre at the patients, scoffing chocolate bars with their parents who, in contrast to their children, had made a great effort to dress well. It was Sunday lunchtime and they looked like they were dressed for an old-fashioned Sunday lunch. The fathers were in suits, the mothers in neat dresses. One unfortunate woman, sitting a few tables away from me, had both her sons in Broadmoor. I saw her lean over and stroke their faces, one after the other.

'I know people are looking out for "nonverbal clues" to my mental state,' Tony continued. 'Psychiatrists love "nonverbal clues". They love to analyse body movements. But that's really hard for the person who is trying to act sane. How do you *sit* in a sane way? How do you *cross your legs* in a sane way? And you know they're really paying attention. So you get self-conscious. You try to smile in a sane way. But it's just . . .' Tony paused. 'It's just . . . *impossible.*'

I suddenly felt quite self-conscious about my own posture. Was I sitting like a journalist? Crossing my legs like a journalist?

'So for a while you thought that being normal and polite would be your ticket out of here,' I said.

'Right,' he replied. 'I volunteered to weed the hospital garden. But they saw how well behaved I was and decided it meant I could only behave well in the environment of a psychiatric hospital and it proved I was mad.'

I glanced suspiciously at Tony. I instinctively didn't

believe him about this. It seemed too *Catch-22*, too darkly-absurd-by-numbers. But later on Tony sent me his files and, sure enough, it was right there.

'Tony is cheerful and friendly', one report stated. 'His detention in hospital is preventing deterioration of his condition.'

(It might seem strange that Tony was allowed to read his medical files, and allowed to pass them on to me, but that's what happened. And, anyway, it was no stranger than the fact that the Scientologists had somehow got me inside Broadmoor, a place where journalists are almost always forbidden. How had they managed it? I had no idea. Maybe they possessed some special, mysterious in or maybe they were just very good at circumventing bureaucracy.)

After Tony read that report, he said, he stopped being well behaved. He started a kind of war of non-cooperation instead. This involved staying in his room a lot. He really wasn't fond of hanging around with rapists and paedophiles anyway. It was unsavoury and also quite frightening. On an earlier occasion, for instance, he had gone into the Stockwell Strangler's room and asked for a cup of lemonade.

'Of course! Take the bottle!' said the Stockwell Strangler.

'Honestly, Kenny, a cup's fine,' said Tony.

'Take the bottle,' he said.

'Really, I just want a cup,' said Tony.

'*TAKE THE BOTTLE!*' hissed the Stockwell Strangler.

On the outside, Tony said, not wanting to spend time with your criminally insane neighbours would be a perfectly understandable position. But on the inside it demonstrates you're withdrawn and aloof and you have a grandiose sense of your own importance. In Broadmoor not wanting to hang out with insane killers is a sign of madness.

'The patient's behaviour is getting worse in Broadmoor,' a report written during Tony's non-cooperation period stated. 'He does not engage [with other patients].'

Then Tony devised a radical new scheme. He stopped talking to the staff too. He realized that if you engage with therapy it's an indication you're getting better, and if you're getting better they have the legal right to detain you, and so if he took no therapy at all he couldn't get better, he'd be untreatable, and they'd have to let him go. (As the law stands in the UK, you cannot indefinitely detain an 'untreatable' patient if their crime was a relatively minor one like GBH.)

The problem was that at Broadmoor if a nurse sits next to you at lunch and makes small talk, and you make small talk back, that's considered engaging with therapy. So Tony had to tell them all, 'Will you sit on another table?'

The psychiatrists realized it was a tactical ploy. They wrote in their reports that it proved him to be 'cunning' and 'manipulative' and also that he was suffering from 'cognitive distortion' because he didn't believe he was mad.

Tony was funny and quite charming for most of my two hours with him, but towards the end he got sadder.

'I arrived here when I was seventeen,' he said. 'I'm twenty-nine now. I've grown up in Broadmoor, wandering the wards of Broadmoor. I've got the Stockwell Strangler on one side of me and the Tiptoe Through The Tulips Rapist on the other. These are supposed to be the best years of your life. I've seen suicides. I saw a man take another man's eye out.'

'How?' I asked.

'With a piece of wood with a nail in it,' said Tony. 'When the guy tried to put his eye back into the socket I had to leave the room.'

Tony said just being there can be enough to turn someone crazy. Then one of the guards called out a word – 'Time' – and with barely a goodbye Tony shot from our table and across the room, to the door that led back to his block. All the patients did the same. It was a display of tremendous, extreme, acute good behaviour. Brian gave me a lift back to the station.

I didn't know what to think. Unlike the sad-eyed, medicated patients all around us, Tony had seemed perfectly ordinary and sane. But what did I know? Brian said it was open and shut. Every day Tony was in Broadmoor was a black day for psychiatry. The sooner they got him out, and Brian was determined to do everything he could, the better it would be.

The next day I wrote to Professor Anthony Maden, the head clinician at Tony's unit at Broadmoor – 'I'm contacting you in the hope that you may be able to shed some light on how true Tony's story might be' – and while I waited for a reply I wondered why Scientology's founder, L. Ron Hubbard, had first decided to create Brian's organization, the CCHR. How did Scientology's war with psychiatry begin? I called Brian.

'You should try over at Saint Hill,' he said. 'They'll probably have some old documents relating to this.'

'Saint Hill?' I said.

'L. Ron Hubbard's old manor house,' Brian said.

Saint Hill Manor – L. Ron Hubbard's home from 1959 to 1966 – stands palatial and impeccably preserved in the East Grinstead countryside, thirty-five miles south of London. There are pristine pillars and priceless twelfth-century Islamic tiles and summer rooms and winter rooms and a room covered from floor to ceiling in a mid-twentieth-century mural of great British public figures portrayed as monkeys – a strange, formally funny satire from long ago commissioned by a previous owner – and a large modern extension, built by Scientology volunteers, in the shape of a medieval castle. Little keepsakes from Hubbard's life, like his cassette recorder and personalized writing paper and a pith helmet, sat on side tables.

I pulled up, assuming Brian would be there to put me in a room so I could quietly study the documents detailing the early days of the Church's war on psychiatry. But as I turned the corner I saw to my surprise that a welcoming committee of some of the world's leading Scientologists had flown thousands of miles with the express purpose of greeting me and showing me around. They were waiting for me on the gravel driveway, dressed in immaculate suits, smiling in anticipation.

• • •

There had been sustained negative media reports about the Church those past weeks and someone high up had clearly decided that I might be the journalist to turn the tide. What had happened was three former high-ranking staff members – Marty Rathbun, Mike Rinder, and Amy Scobee – had a few weeks earlier made some startling accusations against their leader, and L. Ron Hubbard's successor, David Miscavige. They said he routinely punished his top executives for being unsatisfactory Ideas People by slapping them, punching them, 'beating the living fuck' out of them, kicking them when they were on the floor, hitting them in the face, choking them until their faces went purple and unexpectedly forcing them to play an extreme all-night version of musical chairs.

'The fact is,' said the Church's chief spokesperson, Tommy Davis, who had flown from Los Angeles to see me, 'yes, people were hit. Yes, people were kicked while they were on the floor and choked until their faces went purple, but the perpetrator wasn't Mr Miscavige. It was *Marty Rathbun himself*!'

(Marty Rathbun has, I later learnt, admitted to committing those acts of violence, but says he was ordered to by David Miscavige. The Church denies that claim.)

Tommy said that I, unlike most journalists, was a free-thinker, not in the pay of anti-Scientologist vested interests and willing to entertain unexpected realities. He handed me a copy of the in-house Scientology magazine, *Freedom*, which referred to the three people who had made the accusations against David Miscavige as The Kingpin, The Conman, and The Adulteress. The

Adulteress was in fact 'a repeat adulteress' who refused to 'curb her wanton sexual behaviour', perpetrated 'five incidents of extramarital indiscretions' and 'was removed from the Church for ecclesiastical crimes'.

I looked up from the magazine.

'What about the extreme all-night version of musical chairs?' I asked.

There was a short silence.

'Yes, well, Mr Miscavige did make us do that,' said Tommy. 'But it wasn't anywhere near as bad as it was reported. Anyway. Let's give you a tour so we can educate you on what Scientology is really about.'

Tommy handed me over to Bob Keenan, my tour guide. 'I'm L. Ron Hubbard's personal PR rep in the UK,' he said. He was an Englishman, a former firefighter who had, he said, discovered Scientology 'after I broke my back while putting out a fire at a gyppo's flat in East London. There was a donkey in one of the bedrooms. I saw it, turned the corner, and fell through the floor. When I was recovering I read *Dianetics* [Hubbard's self-help book] and it helped me with the pain.'

The manor house was immaculate in a way that manor houses rarely are these days. It was as spotless and sparkling as manor houses in costume dramas set during those long-ago days when the British gentry had real power and unlimited money. The only stain I saw anywhere was in the Winter Room where a small number of the gleaming marble floor tiles were slightly discoloured.

'This is where Ron had his Coca-Cola machine,'

explained Bob. He smiled. 'Ron loved Coca-Cola. He drank it all the time. That was his thing. Anyway, one day the machine leaked some syrup. That's what the stain is. There's been a lot of debate about whether we should clean it up. I say leave it. It's a nice thing.'

'Like a relic,' I said.

'Right,' said Bob.

'A kind of Coca-Cola Turin shroud,' I said.

'Whatever,' said Bob.

Anti-Scientologists believe that the religion and all that is done in its name, including its anti-psychiatry wing, are nothing less than a manifestation of L. Ron Hubbard's madness. They say he was paranoid and depressed (he would apparently at times cry uncontrollably and throw things against the wall and scream). Tommy and Bob said Hubbard was a genius and a great humanitarian. They pointed to his record as a world-class Boy Scout ('The youngest Eagle Scout in America,' said Bob, 'he earned twenty-one merit badges'), pilot, adventurer (the story goes that he once singlehandedly saved a bear from drowning), an incredibly prolific sci-fi author (he could write an entire bestselling novel on a single overnight train journey), philosopher, sailor, guru and whistle-blowing scourge of evil psychiatrists. They say Hubbard was the very first man to reveal that psychiatrists were dosing patients with massive amounts of LSD and elec-tro-convulsive therapy in secret CIA-funded attempts to create brainwashed assassins. He published his account of the experiments in 1969 and it wasn't until June 1975 that the *Washington Post* announced to an unsuspecting world that these programmes (codenamed MK-ULTRA) existed.

> A person drugged and shocked can be ordered to kill and who to kill and how to do it and what to say afterwards. Scientologists, being technically superior to psychiatrists and about a hundred light-years above him morally, object seriously to the official indifference to drug-electric-shock treatments . . . Someday the police will have to take the psychiatrist in hand. The psychiatrist is being found out.
> – L. Ron Hubbard – Pain-Drug-Hypnosis. 1969.

They say Hubbard came to believe that a conspiracy of vested interests, namely the psychiatric and pharmaceutical industries, was behind the political attacks against him because his self-help principles of Dianetics (that we're all laden by 'engrams', painful memories from past lives, and when we clear ourselves of them we can be invincible, we can re-grow teeth, cure blindness, become sane) meant that nobody would ever need to visit a psychiatrist or take an antidepressant again.

A Church video biography of Hubbard's life says: 'L. Ron Hubbard was probably the smartest man that has walked the face of this Earth. We had Jesus, we had Moses, we had Mohammed, all the great people. L. Ron Hubbard is one of this kind.'

The final stop on my guided tour was L. Ron Hubbard's bedroom.

'The very last night he spent in this bed,' Bob said, 'was the night of December 30th 1966. The next night, New Year's Eve, he left England, never to return.'

'Why?' I asked.

'The research he was conducting at the time was just too . . .' Bob fell silent. He gave me a solemn look.

'Are you saying his research was getting just too heavy and he had to leave England in fear for his life?' I asked.

'The conclusions he was coming to . . .' Bob said. An ominous tone had crept into his voice.

'L. Ron Hubbard was never in *fear*,' interjected Tommy Davis, sharply. 'He would never *flee* from anywhere. It wouldn't be right for people to think he *fled*. He only ever did anything on his own terms.'

'He left because he wanted a safe haven,' clarified Bill Walsh, one of the Church's lead attorneys who had flown in from Washington DC to meet me.

'What was the nature of the research?' I asked.

There was a silence. And then Bob quietly said, 'The antisocial personality.'

THE ANTISOCIAL PERSONALITY

[This type of personality] cannot feel any sense of remorse or shame. They approve only of destructive actions. They appear quite rational. They can be *very* convincing.

– L. Ron Hubbard. Introduction to *Scientology Ethics*, 1968.

Hubbard, while living at Saint Hill, began to preach that his enemies, such as the American Psychiatric Association, were Antisocial Personalities, malevolent spirits obsessed with focusing their evil onto him. Their malice had fermented over countless lifetimes, many millions of years, and it was a powerful force indeed. He wrote that it was the duty of every Scientologist to 'ruin them utterly . . . use black propaganda to destroy reputation.' Although he later cancelled the order ('It causes bad public relations,' he wrote) it was this uncompromising attitude – 'We want at least one bad mark on every psychiatrist in England, a murder, an assault, or a rape or more than one . . . There is not one institutional psychiatrist alive who, by ordinary criminal law, could not be arraigned and convicted of extortion, mayhem and murder' – that led to the formation of the anti-psychiatry wing, the CCHR, in 1969.

The CCHR visualized psychiatry as Hubbard had depicted it: as a Dark Empire that had existed for millennia, and themselves as a ragtag rebel force tasked with defeating the Goliath.

And they have won some epic victories. There was, for example, their campaign back in the 1970s and 1980s against the Australian psychiatrist Harry Bailey. He ran a small private suburban psychiatric hospital in Sydney. Patients would turn up suffering from anxiety, depression, schizophrenia, obesity, premenstrual syndrome, and so on. Harry Bailey would greet them and ask them to swallow some tablets. Sometimes the patients knew what was coming, but sometimes they didn't. To those who asked what the pills were for he'd say, 'Oh, it is normal practice.'

So they'd take them, and fall into a deep coma.

Harry Bailey believed that whilst in their comas their minds would cure themselves of whichever mental disorders afflicted them. But somewhere between twenty-six and eighty-five of his patients sank too deep, and died. Some choked on their own vomit, others suffered heart attacks and brain damage and pneumonia and deep-vein thrombosis. The Scientologists eventually got wind of the scandal and set a team onto investigating Bailey, encouraging survivors to sue and the courts to prosecute, which they did, much to Harry Bailey's indignation, who believed his work to be pioneering.

In September 1985, when it became clear he was destined for jail, he wrote a note: 'Let it be known that the Scientologists and the forces of madness have won.' Then he went out to his car and swallowed a bottle of sleeping pills, washed down with beer.

Harry Bailey was dead and hopefully not making use of the afterlife to arm himself with yet more malevolent power to mete out to the human race during some dreadful future lifetime.

When I got home from Saint Hill I watched the CCHR video, *Psychiatry: An Industry of Death*. Much of it is a well-researched catalogue of abuses perpetrated by psychiatrists throughout history. Here was the American physician Samuel Cartwright identifying in 1851 a mental disorder, drapetomania, evident only in slaves. The sole symptom was 'the desire to run away from slavery' and the cure was to 'whip the devil out of them' as a preventative measure. Here was the neurologist Walter Freeman hammering an ice pick through a patient's eye socket sometime during the 1950s. Freeman would travel America in his 'lobotomobile' (a sort of camper-van) enthusiastically lobotomizing wherever he was allowed. Here was behavioural psychologist John Watson spraying a baby with some unidentified clear liquid that I hoped wasn't acid but by that point in the DVD I wouldn't have put anything past those bastards.

But then it veered into speculative territory. Here was Harvard psychologist B. F. Skinner apparently cruelly isolating his baby daughter Deborah in a perspex box for a year. The archive actually captured her looking quite happy in the box and I later did some fact-checking and discovered she's contended throughout her life that the box was basically just a crib and she was hardly ever in there anyway and her father was in fact a lovely man.

The DVD commentary said, 'In every city, every state, every country, you will find psychiatrists committing rape, sexual abuse, murder and fraud.'

A few days later a letter arrived from Tony in Broadmoor. 'This place is awful at night time, Jon,' he wrote. 'Words cannot express the atmosphere. I noticed that the wild daffodils were in bloom this morning. I felt like running through them as I used to in my childhood with my mum.'

Tony had included in the package copies of his files. So I got to read the exact words he used to convince psychiatrists back in 1998 that he was mentally ill. The Dennis Hopper *Blue Velvet* stuff he had told me about was right there – how he liked sending people love letters straight from his heart and a love letter was a bullet from a gun and if you received a love letter from him you'd go straight to hell – but there was a lot more. He'd really gone to town. He told the psychiatrists that the CIA was following him, and that people in the street didn't have real eyes, they had black eyes where their eyes should be, and perhaps the way to make the voices in his head go away was to hurt someone, to take a man hostage and stick a pencil in his eye. He said he was considering stealing an aeroplane because he no longer got a buzz from stealing cars. He said he enjoyed taking things that belonged to other people because he liked the idea of making them suffer. He said hurting people was better than sex.

I wasn't sure which movies those ideas had been taken from. Or even if they had been taken from movies. I felt the ground shift under my feet. Suddenly I was a little on the side of the psychiatrists. Tony must have come over as extremely creepy back then.

There was another page in his file, a description of the crime he committed back in 1997. The victim was a homeless man, an alcoholic called Graham who happened to be sitting on a nearby bench. He apparently made 'an inappropriate comment' about the ten-year-old daughter of one of Tony's friends. The comment was something to do with the length of her dress. Tony told him to shut up. Graham threw a punch at him. Tony retaliated by kicking him. Graham fell over. And that would have been it – Tony later said – had Graham stayed silent. But Graham didn't. Instead he said, 'Is that all you've got?'

Tony 'flipped'. He kicked Graham seven or eight

times in the stomach and groin. He left him, walked back to his friends and had another drink. He then returned to Graham – who was still lying motionless on the ground – bent down and repeatedly head-butted and kicked him again. He kicked him again in the face and walked away.

I remembered that list of movies Tony said he plagiarized to demonstrate he was mentally ill. One was *A Clockwork Orange*, which begins with a gang of thugs kicking a homeless man while he is on the ground.

My phone rang. I recognized the number. It was Tony. I didn't answer it.

A week passed and then the email I had been waiting for arrived. It was from Professor Anthony Maden, the chief clinician at Tony's Dangerous and Severe Personality Disorder unit inside Broadmoor.

'Tony,' his email read, '*did* get here by faking mental illness because he thought it would be preferable to prison.'

He was sure of it, he said, and so were many other psychiatrists who'd met him during the past few years. It was now the consensus. Tony's delusions – the ones he'd presented when he had been on remand in jail – just, in retrospect, didn't ring true. They were too lurid, too clichéd. Plus the minute he was admitted to Broadmoor and looked around and saw what a hellhole he'd got himself into the symptoms vanished.

'Oh!' I thought, pleasantly surprised. 'Good! That's great!'

I had liked Tony when I met him but I'd found myself

feeling warier of him those past days so it was nice to have his story verified by an expert.

But then I read Professor Maden's next line: 'Most psychiatrists who have assessed him, and there have been a lot, have considered he is not mentally ill, but suffers from psychopathy.'

I looked at the email. 'Tony's a *psychopath*?' I thought.

I didn't know very much at all about psychopaths back then, only the story James told me about Essi Viding when I was solving the *Being or Nothingness* mystery: 'She showed him a picture of a frightened face and asked him to identify the emotion. He said he didn't know what the emotion was but it was the face people pulled just before he killed them.' So I didn't know much about psychopaths, but I did know this: it sounded worse.

I emailed Professor Maden: 'Isn't that like that scene in the movie *Ghost* when Whoopi Goldberg pretends to be a psychic and then it turns out that she actually can talk to the dead?'

'No,' he emailed back. 'It isn't like that Whoopi Goldberg scene. Tony faked mental illness. That's when you have hallucinations and delusions. Mental illness comes and goes. It can get better with medication. Tony is a psychopath. That doesn't come and go. It is how the person is.'

Faking mental illness to get out of a prison sentence, he explained, is exactly the kind of deceitful and manipulative act you'd expect of a psychopath. Tony faking his brain going wrong was a sign that his brain had gone wrong.

'There is no doubt about Tony's diagnosis,' his email concluded.

Tony rang again. I didn't answer.

'Classic psychopath!' said Essi Viding.

There was a silence.

'Really?' I asked.

'Yeah!' she said. 'How he turned up to meet you! It's classic psychopath!'

After I received my email from Professor Maden I called Essi to see if she'd meet me. I had just told her about the moment I'd first seen Tony, how he had strolled purposefully across the Broadmoor Wellness Centre in a pinstripe suit, like someone from *The Apprentice*, his arm outstretched.

'*That's* classic psychopath?' I asked.

'I was visiting a psychopath in prison one time,' Essi said. 'I'd read his dossier. He'd had a horrific history of raping women and killing them and biting their nipples off. It was just hideous, harrowing reading. Another psychologist said to me, "You'll meet this guy and you'll be totally charmed by him." I thought, "No way!" And you know what? *Totally!* To the point that I found him a little bit fanciable. He was really good looking, in peak physical condition, and a very macho manner. It was raw sex appeal. I could completely understand why the women he had killed went with him.'

'The idea that wearing a sharp suit might be an indication that the guy's a psychopath,' I said. 'Where does that come from?'

'The Hare Checklist,' said Essi. 'The PCL-R.'

I looked blankly at her.

'It's a kind of psychopath test designed by a Canadian psychologist called Bob Hare,' she said. 'It's the gold standard for diagnosing psychopaths. The first item on the checklist is "Glibness/Superficial charm".'

Essi told me a little about Bob Hare's psychopath test. From the way she described it, it sounded quite odd. She said you can go on a course where Hare himself teaches you ways of stealthily spotting psychopaths by reading suspects' body language and the nuances of their sentence construction, etc.

'How old is Tony?' she asked.

'Twenty-nine,' I said.

'Well, good luck to Professor Maden,' she said. 'I don't think his offending days are over.'

'How do you *know* this?' I asked.

Suddenly Essi seemed to me like a brilliant wine-taster, identifying a rare wine through spotting the barely discernible clues. Or maybe she was like a clever vicar, believing wholeheartedly in something too imperceptible ever to prove.

'Psychopaths don't change,' she said. 'They don't learn from punishment. The best you can hope for is that they'll eventually get too old and lazy to be bothered to offend. And they can seem impressive. Charismatic. People are dazzled. So, yeah, the real trouble starts when one makes it big in mainstream society.'

I told Essi that I'd seen how Petter Nordlund's crazy book had briefly messed up her colleagues' hitherto rational worlds. Of course there was nothing at all psychopathic about Petter – he seemed anxious and obsessive, just like I was, albeit quite a lot more so. But as a result of the *Being or Nothingness* adventure I'd become fascinated to learn about the influence that madness – madness amongst our leaders – had on our everyday lives. Did Essi really believe that many of them really are ill with Tony's condition? Are many of them psychopaths?

She nodded. 'With prison psychopaths you can actually quantify the havoc they cause,' she said. 'They make up only twenty-five per cent of the prison population but they account for sixty to seventy per cent of the violent crime that happens inside prisons. They're few in number but you don't want to mess with them.'

'What percentage of the non-prison population is a psychopath?' I asked.

'One per cent,' said Essi.

Essi said if I wanted to understand what a psychopath is, and how they sometimes rise to the top of the business world, I should seek out the writings of Bob Hare, the father of modern psychopathy research. Tony will no doubt be incarcerated because he scored high on the Bob Hare checklist, she said.

And so, after I left her office, I found an article by Hare that described psychopaths as 'predators who use charm, manipulation, intimidation, sex and violence to control others and to satisfy their own selfish needs. Lacking in conscience and empathy, they take what they want and do as they please, violating social norms and expectations without guilt or remorse. What is missing, in other words, are the very qualities that allow a human being to live in social harmony.'

• • •

Tony called. I couldn't keep ignoring him. I took a breath and picked up the phone.

'Jon?' he said.

He sounded small and far away and echoey. I imagined him on a payphone halfway down a long corridor.

'Yes, hello, Tony,' I said, in a no-nonsense way.

'I haven't heard from you in a while,' said Tony.

He sounded like a child whose parents had suddenly started acting frostily for no obvious reason.

'Professor Maden says you're a psychopath,' I said.

Tony exhaled, impatiently.

'I'm not a psychopath,' he said.

There was a short silence.

'How do you know?' I asked.

'They say psychopaths can't feel remorse,' said Tony. 'I feel lots of remorse. But when I tell them I feel remorse they say psychopaths pretend to be remorseful when they're not.' Tony paused. 'It's like witchcraft,' he said. 'They turn everything upside down.'

'What makes them believe you're a psychopath?' I said.

'Ah,' said Tony. 'Back in 1998 when I was faking mental illness I stupidly included some fake psychopathic stuff in there. Like Ted Bundy. Remember I plagiarized a Ted Bundy book? Ted Bundy was definitely a psychopath. I think that's the problem.'

'OK,' I said. I sounded unconvinced.

'Trying to prove you're not a psychopath is even harder than trying to prove you're not mentally ill,' said Tony.

'How did they diagnose you?' I asked.

'They give you a psychopath test,' said Tony. 'The Robert Hare Checklist. They assess you for twenty personality traits. They go down a list. Superficial Charm. Proneness to Boredom. Lack of Empathy. Lack of Remorse. Grandiose Sense of Self-Worth. That sort of thing. For each one they score you a 0, 1 or 2. If your total score is thirty or more out of forty, you're a psychopath. That's it. You're doomed. You're labelled a psychopath for life. They say you can't change. You can't be treated. You're a danger to society. And then you're stuck somewhere like *this* . . .'

Tony's voice rose in anger and frustration. I heard it bounce across the walls of the DSPD unit. Then he controlled himself and lowered his voice again.

'And then you're stuck somewhere like this,' he said. 'If I'd just done my time in prison I'd have been out seven years ago.'

'Tell me more about the psychopath test,' I said to Tony.

'One of the questions they ask you to assess you for Irresponsibility is "Do you mix with criminals?" Of *course* I mix with criminals. I am in bloody *Broadmoor*.'

He clearly had a point. But, still, Brian knew he and Tony were in danger of losing me. He called and asked if I wanted to visit Tony one last time. He said he had a question he wanted to spring on him and he wanted me to hear it. And so the three of us spent another Sunday lunchtime eating chocolate and drinking PG Tips in the Broadmoor Wellness Centre.

Tony wasn't wearing the pinstripe this time, but he was still by far the best-dressed potential sufferer of a dangerous and severe personality disorder in the room.

We made small talk for a while. I told him I wanted to change his name for this story. I asked him to choose a name. We decided on Tony. Tony said knowing his luck they'd read this and diagnose him with Dissociative Identity Disorder.

Then, suddenly, Brian leaned forward.

'Do you feel remorse?' he asked.

'My remorse,' Tony instantly replied, leaning forward too, 'is that I've not only screwed up my victims' life but also my own life and my family's lives and that's my remorse. All the things that could have been done in my life. I feel bad about that every day.'

Tony looked at me.

Did his remorse sound a bit rattled off? I thought. I looked at Tony. Did they rehearse this? Was this a show for me? And, also, if he *really* felt remorse, wouldn't he have said, 'My remorse that I've not only screwed up my life but also my victims' life . . .'? Wouldn't he have put his statement of remorse in that order? Or maybe it *was* in the right order. I didn't know. Should I want him released? Shouldn't I? How could I know? It crossed my mind that perhaps I should be campaigning for his release in print in a way that *appeared* crusading but actually wasn't quite effective enough to work. Like planting barely noticeable seeds of doubt into the prose. Subtle.

I felt myself narrow my eyes, as if I was trying to bore a hole through Tony's skull and peer into his brain. The look of concentrated curiosity on my face was the same look I had back at that Costa Coffee when Deborah first slid her copy of *Being or Nothingness* over to me. Tony and Brian could tell what was going through my mind. The two men leaned back in disappointment.

'You're sitting there like an amateur sleuth trying to read between the lines,' said Brian.

'I am,' I nodded.

'That's all psychiatrists do!' said Brian. 'See? They're nothing but amateur sleuths too! But they've got the power to influence parole boards. To get someone like Tony locked away indefinitely if he has the misfortune to fail Bob Hare's psychopath checklist!'

And then our two hours were up, and a guard called time, and with barely a goodbye Tony obediently rushed across the Wellness Centre and was gone.

3

PSYCHOPATHS DREAM
IN BLACK AND WHITE

It was the French psychiatrist Philippe Pinel who first suggested, early in the nineteenth century, that there was a madness that didn't involve mania or depression or psychosis. He called it 'manie sans delire' – insanity without delusions. He said sufferers appeared normal on the surface but they lacked impulse controls and were prone to outbursts of violence. It wasn't until 1891, when the German doctor J. L. A. Koch published his book *Die psychopathischen Minderwertigkeiten*, that it got its name: Psychopathy.

Back in the old days – in the days before Bob Hare – the definitions were rudimentary. The 1959 Mental Health Act for England and Wales described psychopaths simply as having 'a persistent disorder or disability of mind (whether or not including subnormality of intelligence) which results in abnormally aggressive or seriously irresponsible conduct on the part of the patient, and requires or is susceptible to medical treatment.'

The consensus from the beginning was that only one per cent of humans had it but the chaos they caused was so far-reaching it could actually re-mould society, re-mould it all wrong, like when someone breaks their foot and it's cast badly and the bones stick out in odd directions. And so the urgent question became, how could psychopaths be cured?

In the late 1960s a young Canadian psychiatrist believed he had the answer. His name was Elliott Barker. His strange story has all but faded away now besides making the odd fleeting cameo – a once beautiful but now broken 1960s star – in the obituary of some hopeless Canadian serial killer, but back then his peer group was watching his experiments with great excitement. He looked to be on the cusp of something extraordinary.

I happened to come across references to him in academic papers I read during the weeks after I visited Tony in Broadmoor, and Essi Viding, and was trying to understand the meaning of psychopathy. There were allusions to his warm-spiritedness, his childlike, if odd, idealism, his willingness to journey to the furthest corners of his imagination in his attempts to cure psychopaths. These were phrases I hadn't seen anywhere else in reports about psychiatric initiatives inside asylums for the criminally insane and so I began sending emails to him and his friends.

'Elliott lies very low and does not grant any interviews,' emailed a former colleague of his, who didn't want to be named. 'He is a sweet man who to this day has a lot of enthusiasm for helping people.'

'I know of nothing comparable to what Elliott Barker did,' emailed another, Richard Weisman, a social science professor at York University in Toronto, who wrote a brilliant paper on him – 'Reflections on the Oak Ridge Experiment with Mentally Disordered Offenders' – for the *International Journal of Law and Psychiatry*. 'It was a unique synthesis of a number of different cultural trends in the '60s in Canada and Elliott was lucky to have a remarkably free hand in his improvisations.'

I became quite obsessed with piecing together the Oak Ridge story. I fired off emails to no avail: 'Dear Elliott, I never usually persevere so much and please accept my apologies for doing so,' and 'Is there anything I can do to convince you to talk to me?' and 'I promise this will be my last email if I don't hear from you!'

And then I had a stroke of luck. Whilst other prospective interviewees might have found my somewhat fanatical determination odd, perhaps even unnerving, Elliott and his fellow former Oak Ridge psychiatrists found it appealing, and the more I hassled them the more they were quietly warming to me. Finally, they began to open up and answer my emails.

It all started in the mid-1960s. Elliott Barker was a budding psychiatrist back then, just out of college. While trying to decide which career path to take he began reading in psychiatry magazines about the emergence of radical Therapeutic Communities where the old hierarchies of the wise therapist and the incompetent patient had been torn down and replaced with something more experimental. Intrigued, he and his young wife took a bank loan and set off on a year-long round-the-world odyssey to visit as many of these places as they could.

In Palm Springs, California, he heard about Nude Psychotherapy sessions occurring under the tutelage of a psychotherapist named Paul Bindrim. The hotel the sessions took place in combined (as its advertising material back then stated) 'abundant trees and wildlife' with the facilities of a 'high class resort'. There, Bindrim would ask his fully clothed clients, who were strangers to one another and usually middle- to upper-class Californian free-thinkers and movie stars, first to 'eyeball' each other, and then hug, and wrestle, and then, in the dark, and to the accompaniment of new age music, to remove their 'tower of clothes'. They would sit naked in a circle, perform a 'meditation-like hum', and then dive headlong into a marathon twenty-four-hour nonstop Nude Psychotherapy session, an emotional and mystical rollercoaster during which participants would scream and yell and sob and confess their innermost fears and anxieties.

'Physical nakedness,' Bindrim would explain to visiting journalists, 'facilitates emotional nakedness and therefore speeds up psychotherapy.'

Bindrim's most divisive idea was what he termed Crotch Eyeballing. He'd instruct a participant to sit in the centre of the circle with their legs in the air. Then he'd command the others to stare at that person's genitals and anus, sometimes for hours, while he sporadically yelled, 'This is where it's at! This is where we are so damned negatively conditioned!'

A Paul Bindrim Nude Psychotherapy Session
photographed by Ralph Crane on 1 December 1968.

Sometimes he'd direct participants to address their genitals directly. One journalist who attended a session – *Life* magazine's Jane Howard – reported in her 1970 book *Please Touch: A Guided Tour of the Human Potential Movement* a conversation between Bindrim and a participant called Lorna.

'Tell Katy what things happen in your crotch,' Bind-rim ordered her. Katy was Lorna's vagina. 'Say, "Katy, this is where I shit, fuck, piss and masturbate." '

There was an embarrassed silence.

'I think Katy already *knows* that,' Lorna eventually replied.

Many travellers around the Californian Human Potential movement considered Nude Psychotherapy to be a step too far but Elliott, on his odyssey, found the idea exhilarating.

Elliott's odyssey took him onwards, to Turkey and Greece and West Berlin and East Berlin and Japan and Korea and Hong Kong. His most inspiring day occurred in London when (he told me by email) he 'met with [the legendary radical psychiatrists] RD Laing and DG Cooper and visited Kingsley Hall, their therapeutic community for schizophrenics.'

As it happened, R. D. Laing's son Adrian runs a law firm just a few streets away from my home in North London. And so – in my quest to understand Elliott's influences – I called in to ask if he'd tell me something about Kingsley Hall.

Adrian Laing is a slight, trim man. He has the face of his father but on a less daunting body.

'The point about Kingsley Hall,' he said, 'was that people could go there and work through their mad-ness. My father believed that if you allowed madness to take its natural course without intervention – without lobotomies and drugs and strait-jackets and all the awful things they were doing at the time in mental hospitals –

it would burn itself out, like an LSD trip working its way through the system.'

'What kind of thing might Elliott Barker have seen on his visit to Kingsley Hall?' I asked.

'Some rooms were, you know, beguilingly draped in Indian silks,' Adrian said. 'Schizophrenics like Ian Spurling – who eventually became Freddie Mercury's costume designer – would dance and sing and paint and recite poetry and rub shoulders with visiting free-thinking celebrities like Timothy Leary and Sean Connery.' Adrian paused. 'And then there were other, less beguiling rooms, like Mary Barnes's shit room down in the basement.'

'Mary Barnes's shit room?' I asked. 'You mean like the worst room in the house?'

'I was seven when I first visited Kingsley Hall,' Adrian said. 'My father said to me, "There's a very special person down in the basement who wants to meet you." So I went down there and the first thing I said was, "What's that smell of shit?" '

The smell of shit was – Adrian told me – coming from a chronic schizophrenic called Mary Barnes. She represented a conflict at Kingsley Hall. Laing held madness in great esteem. He believed the insane possessed a special knowledge – only they understood the true madness that permeated society. But Mary Barnes, down in the basement, hated being mad. It was agony for her, and she desperately wanted to be normal.

Her needs won out. Laing and his fellow Kingsley Hall psychiatrists encouraged her to regress to the infantile state in the hope that she might grow up once again, but sane. The plan wasn't going well. She was constantly naked, smearing herself and the walls in her own excreta, communicating only by squeals and refusing to eat unless someone fed her from a bottle.

'The smell of Mary Barnes's shit was proving a real ideological problem,' Adrian said. 'They used to have long discussions about it. Mary needed to be free to roll around in her own shit but the smell of it would impinge upon other people's freedom to smell fresh air. So they spent a lot of time trying to formulate a shit policy.'

'And what about your father?' I asked. 'What was he like in the midst of all this?'

Adrian coughed. 'Well,' he said, 'the downside of having no barriers between doctors and patients was that everyone became a patient.'

There was a silence. 'When I envisaged Kingsley Hall I imagined everyone becoming a doctor,' I said. 'I suppose I was feeling quite optimistic about humanity.'

'Nope,' Adrian said. 'Everyone became a patient. Kingsley Hall was very wild. There was an unhealthy respect for madness there. The first thing my father did was lose himself completely, go crazy, because there was a part of him that *was* totally fucking mad. In his case, it was a drunken, wild madness.'

'That's an incredibly depressing thought,' I said, 'that if you're in a room and at one end lies madness and at the other end lies sanity it is human nature to veer towards the madness end.'

Adrian nodded. He said visitors like Elliott Barker would have been kept away from the darkest corners, like Mary Barnes' shit room and his father's drunken insanity, and instead steered towards the Indian silks and the delightful poetry evenings with Sean Connery in attendance.

'By the way,' I said, 'did they ever manage to formulate a successful shit policy?'

'Yes,' Adrian said. 'One of my dad's colleagues said, "She wants to paint with her shit. Maybe we should give her *paints*." And it worked.'

Mary Barnes eventually became a celebrated and much-exhibited artist. Her paintings were greatly admired throughout the 1960s and 1970s for illustrating the mad, colourful, painful, exuberant, complicated inner life of a schizophrenic.

'And it got rid of the smell of shit,' Adrian said.

Elliott Barker returned from London, his head a jumble of radical ideas garnered from his odyssey, and applied for work at a unit for psychopaths inside the Oak Ridge Hospital for the Criminally Insane in Ontario. Impressed by the details of his great journey, the hospital board offered him a job.

The psychopaths he met during his first days at Oak Ridge were nothing like R. D. Laing's schizophrenics. Although they were undoubtedly insane you would never realize it. They *seemed* perfectly ordinary. This, Elliott deduced, was because they were burying their insanity deep beneath a facade of normality. If the madness could only, somehow, be brought to the surface maybe it would work itself through and they could be reborn as empathetic human beings. The alternative was stark: unless their personalities could be radically altered, these young men were destined for a lifetime of incarceration.

And so he successfully sought permission from the Canadian government to obtain a large batch of LSD (acquiring it from a government-sanctioned lab, Connaught Laboratories, University of Toronto), handpicked a group of psychopaths ('They have been selected on the basis of verbal ability and most are relatively young and intelligent offenders between 17 and 25,' he explained in the October 1968 issue of the *Canadian Journal of Corrections*), led them into what he named the Total Encounter Capsule, a small room painted bright green, and asked them to remove their clothes. This was truly to be a radical milestone: the world's first ever marathon Nude Psychotherapy session for criminal psychopaths.

Elliott's raw, naked, LSD-fuelled sessions lasted for epic eleven-day stretches. The psychopaths spent every waking moment journeying to their darkest corners in an attempt to get better. There were no distractions – no television, no clothes, no clocks, no calendars, only a perpetual discussion (at least a hundred hours every week) of their feelings. When they got hungry they sucked food through straws that protruded through the walls. Much like during Paul Bindrim's own Nude Psychotherapy sessions, they were encouraged to go to their rawest emotional places by screaming and clawing at the walls and confessing fantasies of forbidden sexual longing for each other even if they were, in the words of an internal Oak Ridge report of the time, 'in a state of arousal while doing so'.

My guess is that this would have been a more enjoyable experience within the context of a Palm Springs resort hotel than a secure facility for psychopathic murderers.

Elliott himself was absent, watching it all from behind a one-way mirror. He would not be the one to treat the psychopaths. They would tear down the bourgeois constructs of traditional psychotherapy and be each other's psychiatrists.

There were some inadvertently weird touches. For instance, visitors to the unit were an unavoidable inconvenience. There would be tour groups of local teenagers: a government initiative to demystify asylums. This caused Elliott a problem. How could he ensure the presence of strangers wouldn't puncture the radical atmosphere he'd spent months creating? And then he had a brainwave. He acquired some particularly grisly crime-scene photographs of people who had committed suicide in gruesome ways, by shooting themselves in the face, for instance, and he hung them around the visitors' necks. Now everywhere the psychopaths looked they would be confronted by the dreadful reality of violence.

Elliott's early reports were gloomy. The atmosphere inside the Capsule was tense. Psychopaths would stare angrily at each other. Days would go by when nobody would exchange a word. Some non-cooperative prisoners especially resented being forced by their fellow psychopaths to attend a subprogramme where they had to intensively discuss their reasons for not wanting to intensively discuss their feelings. Others took exception to being forced to wear little-girl-type dresses (a psychopath-devised punishment for non-cooperation in the programme). Plus, nobody liked glancing up and seeing some teenager peering curiously through the window at them with a giant crime-scene photograph dangling around their neck. The whole thing, for all the good intentions, looked doomed to failure.

• • •

I managed to track down one former Oak Ridge inmate who had been invited by Elliott to join the programme. Nowadays Steve Smith runs a Plexiglas business in Vancouver. He's had a successful and ordinary life. But back in the late 1960s he was a teenage drifter, incarcerated for thirty days at Oak Ridge in the winter of 1968 after he was caught stealing a car whilst tripping on LSD.

'I remember Elliott Barker coming into my cell,' Steve told me. 'He was charming, soothing. He put his arm around my shoulder. He called me Steve. It was the first time anyone had used my first name in there. He asked me if I thought I was mentally ill. I said I thought I wasn't. "Well, I'll tell you," he said, "I think you are a very slick psychopath. I want you to know that there are people just like you in here who have been locked up more than twenty years. But we have a program here that can help you get over your illness." So there I was, only eighteen at the time, I'd stolen a car so I wasn't exactly the criminal of the century, locked in a padded room for eleven days with a bunch of psychopaths, the lot of us high on scopolamine [a type of hallucinogenic] and they were all staring at me.'

'What did they say to you?'

'That they were there to help me.'

'What's your single most vivid memory of your days inside the programme?' I asked Steve.

'I went in and out of delirium,' he said. 'One time, when I regained consciousness, I saw that they'd strapped me to Peter Woodcock.'

'Who's Peter Woodcock?' I asked.

'Look him up on Wikipedia,' he said.

Peter Woodcock (born March 5, 1939) is a Canadian serial killer and child rapist who murdered three young children in Toronto, Canada in 1956 and 1957 when he was still a teenager. Woodcock was apprehended in 1957, declared legally insane and placed in Oak Ridge, an Ontario psychiatric facility located in Penetanguishene.

Wikipedia

'That does sound unpleasant,' I said. 'Oh. I've just found a video interview with him.'

PETER WOODCOCK: I regret that children died, but I felt like God. It was the power of God over a human being.

INTERVIEWER: Why was that important to you?

WOODCOCK: It was the pleasure it gave me. I got very little pleasure from anything else in life. But in the strangling of children I found a degree and a sensation of pleasure. And of accomplishment. Because it was such a good feeling I wanted to duplicate it. And so I went out to seek duplication.

INTERVIEWER: People would be horrified to hear you view it as an accomplishment.

WOODCOCK: I know, but I'm sorry, this is not meant for sensitive ears. This is a terrible recitation. I'm being as honest as I can.

– BBC documentary, *The Mask of Sanity*

'Why were you strapped to Peter Woodcock?' I asked Steve.

'He was my "buddy", making sure I got through the drug trip safely.'

'What did he say to you?'

'That he was there to help me.'

That was all Steve said about his time with Peter Woodcock. He depicted it as a fleeting hallucinatory nightmare. But a few months later, in March 2010, when I emailed Steve to ask if he'd heard the news that Woodcock had just died, he replied: 'That makes my skin crawl. God damn! You see, I have a deep but unwanted connection with that monster. We had matching small flower tattoos on both our right forearms. We did it together – typical jail house tattoos.'

Getting a matching tattoo with a multiple-child-killer was just the kind of twisted thing that happened inside the Oak Ridge Capsule, Steve said, where nothing made sense, where reality got malformed through LSD, where psychopaths all around you were clawing at the walls, where everyone was suffering sleep deprivation, and Elliott Barker was watching it all from behind a one-way mirror.

But then, as the weeks turned into months, something unexpected began to happen. The transformation was captured by a CBC documentary maker, Norm Perry, who was invited into Oak Ridge by Elliott in 1971. It is an incredibly moving film. These tough young prisoners are, before our eyes, changing. They are learning to care for one another inside the Capsule.

'I love the way you talk,' one prisoner tells another. There is real tenderness in his voice. 'You just let it flow from you as if you own all the words in the world. They're your personal property and you make them dance for you.'

We see Elliott in his office, and the look of delight on his face is quite heart-breaking. He's trying to conceal it, trying to adopt an air of professionalism, but you can tell. His psychopaths have become gentle. Some are even telling their parole boards not to consider them for release until after they've completed their therapy. The authorities are astonished. Patients never request *not* to be let out.

By the mid-1970s, the milieu at Oak Ridge became, if anything, a little *too* beautiful. This was when Elliott – tired and a bit burned out and wanting a break – stepped down for a while and a prodigy, a young psychiatrist named Gary Maier, took the helm. Oak Ridge staff were quite taciturn on the subject of what had occurred under Gary Maier's stewardship. 'He was no Elliot that was for sure,' emailed one staff member, who didn't want to be named. 'Whereas Elliot to all appearances was a conservative-looking fellow in spite of the outlandish treatment ideas, Gary was a long-haired sandal-clad hippy.'

Nowadays Gary Maier lives in Madison, Wisconsin. He's semi-retired but still practises psychiatry at two maximum-security prisons there. When I met him for breakfast at the Ambassador Hotel in downtown Milwaukee he told me how he first heard about Elliott's

programme. It was at a government-sponsored recruitment seminar for psychiatry graduates. Barry Boyd, who
ran Oak Ridge, was one of the speakers. He eulogized
Elliott to the audience and recounted their many success
stories.

'Like Matt Lamb,' Gary said. 'This Matt Lamb
fellow had apparently killed people . . .' (The nineteen
-year-old Matt Lamb had been hiding behind a tree
near a bus stop in Windsor, Ontario, in January
1967, when a group of young people walked past. He
jumped out from behind the tree and without saying a word shot them all. Two of them, a twenty-year-
old woman and a twenty-one-year-old man, died.)
'. . . And when they asked him what it was like to kill
those strangers he said it was like squashing bugs. He was
one of Elliott's – I wouldn't want to say *all-stars* – but he
had about as cold a personality as psychopaths have
and he really seemed to warm up and benefit from the
program.'

When Barry Boyd recounted the Matt Lamb story
at the recruitment seminar some of the psychiatry graduates gasped to hear that he was now a free man, declared cured in 1973, a Capsule success story, and was
living with Elliott and his family at their farm, spending his days peacefully whitewashing fences and
pondering his future. He had stayed trouble-free, but
the consensus was that psychopaths invariably lapsed
into chaos. Inviting Matt Lamb to live with him was a
huge leap of faith, like a lion-tamer sharing a house with
his lion.

But Gary didn't gasp. He clasped his hands in delight. At the end of the night he approached Barry Boyd.

'If there's ever a job going at Oak Ridge . . .' he told him.

As it happened, Elliott was searching for a collaborator and a few weeks later they offered it to Gary.

That evening Gary had a spontaneous out-of-body experience. He took it as a sign that it was *right*.

'And how did you feel on your first day at work?' I asked.

'I felt like I was *home*,' Gary said.

Gary has the thick, muscular body of a prison guard but the goatee and kind eyes of a sixty-seven-year-old hippy. He said he saw the men at Oak Ridge back then as searching souls with kind hearts, just like he was. He gazed into their eyes and he didn't fear them.

'When you gaze into the eyes of another person you can only see as far as his closed door,' he said. 'So take it as an opportunity to knock on that door. If he doesn't want to open the door you bow to him and you say, "That's fine. When you're ready." '

'What would be behind their closed doors?' I asked.

'Freedom,' said Gary.

And there *was* freedom at Oak Ridge, Gary said, freedom everywhere: 'One guy had a real liking for another guy who lived in a different ward. He'd see him in the yard. So he'd simply leave his body, walk through the walls, make love to the guy, and then come back to his cell. We all said he should feel free to continue to do it as long as he was gentle. He kept me personally appraised of their lovemaking. I have no idea what that other fellow experienced.' Gary laughed, sadly. 'I haven't had that memory for a long time,' he said.

They were the best days of Gary's life. He knew how to make these men well.

'I honestly believe I was doing a job that most Canadian psychiatrists couldn't do,' he said. And the hospital administrators had faith enough in him to allow him to take his psychopaths on a journey into uncharted waters. Like the Dream Group.

'People dream and I wanted to capture what was going on in their dreams,' Gary said. 'So before they went to bed I'd have them hold hands and say, "Let me experience my dream life in this community." And then they would quietly go to sleep, and dream.'

When they awoke they'd head straight to the dream group, which consisted of an equal number of psychopaths and schizophrenics.

'The problem,' Gary said, 'was that the schizophrenics had incredibly vivid dreams – dream after dream after dream – but the psychopaths would be lucky if they even *had* a dream.'

'Why do schizophrenics dream more than psychopaths?' I asked.

'I don't know,' Gary laughed. 'I do remember the schizophrenics usually dreamt in colour – the more intense a dream the more likely it's going to be in colour – but the psychopaths, if they managed to have a dream at all, dreamt in black and white.'

All this was creating a power imbalance. In regular

groups meetings, Gary said, the schizophrenics would be subservient to the psychopaths, 'but suddenly the poor psychopaths had to sit and listen to the schizophrenics go on about dream one, dream two, dream three . . .'

When it was time for the patients to vote on whether to continue the dream group, the schizophrenics said yes, but the psychopaths vociferously argued against it, and were victorious.

'Just because of the power struggle?' I asked.

'Well, there was that,' said Gary, 'plus who wants to listen to some schizophrenic's boring dream?'

Then there was the mass chanting.

'We'd do it after lunch. We chanted Om for maybe twenty-five minutes. It was so pleasurable for the guys. The ward sounded like sort of an echo chamber, and pretty soon they started to chant Om in harmony.' Gary paused. 'We used to have visiting psychiatrists. One day one of them was sitting in on the chant when she suddenly jumped up and ran from the room. It was quite an embarrassment. We found her out in the corridor. She said, "Being in that room was like a freight train coming to run me over. I just had to get out of it." '

'She panicked?'

'She panicked,' Gary said. 'She thought she'd lose control and would somehow be attacked.'

Gary's most vivid Oak Ridge memories involved gentle psychopaths learning and growing but foolish psychiatrists and security guards conspiring to spoil everything. Which is exactly, he said, what happened when it all went too far, when it all went somewhat *Heart of Darkness*.

> Concern has been expressed as to the direction
> of recent developments in treatment. The use of
> LSD appears to be undergoing some change from
> the approach originally approved [along with] the
> introduction of mystical concepts. I would ask
> you to gently de-escalate these aspects of your
> program.
>   – Memo from Oak Ridge Medical Director
>   Barry Boyd to Gary Maier, August 11th 1975.

'OK, you saw that memo,' said Gary. 'Ah.'
'What happened?'
Gary let out a sigh. 'Right . . .' he began.

Gary asked me to consider what happens when any of us – no matter what age we are – go home to visit our parents at Christmas. It doesn't matter how wise and insightful adult life has made us, 'Two days with your parents at Christmas and you'll all just be swatted back to the deepest level of the family's pathology.'

He had that exact same problem at Oak Ridge. 'We'd give these guys LSD. They'd have these marathon weekends, and they'd *change*, but then they'd go back to a general ward that wasn't *ready* for the change. So they'd be swatted right back.'

Two steps forward, two steps back. If only the entire general ward – every psychopath in the whole place – could somehow achieve metaphysical enlightenment at the same time . . .

And then it came to him: a mass LSD trip! It was radical but critical, the only way to break down the deep pathology of the ward.

'I saw it as the culmination of all the stuff I had done,' Gary said. 'Give everyone the rite of passage of LSD at the same time. Or over a few days. Well, that was very upsetting for the security staff. They came into work and I said to them, "Just leave the guys alone." '

And so the guards, bristling with anger and uncertainty, were forced to stand back as twenty-six serial killers and rapists ran around, en masse, off their heads on LSD.

'I probably didn't play my cards properly there,' Gary said. 'I think the guards lost their identity. The union guys probably thought I was going to get people fired . . .'

A few days later Gary received the warning memo, and a few days after that he turned up for work to discover that his keys no longer fitted the locks. The guards had changed them overnight. One told him – from the other side of the bars – that he was fired and he could never set foot in Oak Ridge again.

'Oh well,' Gary said now, pushing what was left of his breakfast across his plate, 'I was ready to move on.'

During the years that followed Gary's departure, Elliott Barker continued to win over fans from across the criminal-psychiatry community. Maybe he really had achieved something nobody had managed before: 'For the first thirty years of Oak Ridge no one charged with a capital offence was ever released from here,' he told the documentary maker Norm Perry. 'But there is real hope now that patients are breaking out of their psychological prison of indifference to the feelings of others, a prison that to a greater or lesser extent confines us all. We are making people well again – people who killed or raped while mentally ill – we are making them well and able to be safe and useful members of society.'

Elliott's best friends in the world were, he'd tell his neighbours, ex-Oak Ridge patients. His father was a violent alcoholic who beat his family and committed suicide when Elliott was ten. I wondered whether that was why he'd dedicated his life to teaching psychopaths to be tender. And patients were indeed released from Oak Ridge. Elliott kept in touch with many, inviting them to stay at his farm in Midland, Ontario, where they played racquetball together and built fences and planted crops.

Back home in London, as I began to piece this story together, I was bowled over by Elliott's accomplishments. I felt terribly sorry for Tony, trapped in Broadmoor. So many psychopathic murderers – fortunate to have been under Elliott and Gary's radical tutelage – had been declared cured and freed. Why couldn't Broadmoor adopt some of Elliott's ideas? Of course they seemed hokey and dated and naive and perhaps overly reliant on hallucinogenics, but they were surely preferable to locking someone up forever because he happened to score badly on some personality checklist.

• • •

I learnt that, fascinatingly, two researchers had in the early 1990s undertaken a detailed study of the long-term recidivism rates of psychopaths who'd been through Elliott's programme and let out into society. Its publication would surely have been an extraordinary moment for Elliott and Gary and the Capsule. In regular circumstances sixty per cent of criminal psychopaths released into the outside world go on to reoffend. What percentage of their psychopaths had?

As it turned out: eighty per cent.

The Capsule had made the psychopaths *worse*.

One, Cecil Gilles, was declared cured and released after many intensive therapeutic months. Within days he had grabbed at random a fourteen-year-old girl, sexually assaulted her and thrown her, unconscious, from a bridge into a creek. She managed to crawl to a nearby house and in through a window where she was found later that night lying on the kitchen floor. She survived but suffered severe scars from where her head had hit the floor of the creek.

Another, Joseph Fredericks, was released from Oak Ridge in 1983 and within weeks had attacked a teenage girl with a knife and sodomized a ten-year-old boy. He was released again a year later and attacked an eleven-year old boy. Four years after that he was released and headed to a mall called Shoppers World where he abducted and raped an eleven-year-old boy called Christopher Stephenson. The boy wrote a note to his parents:

'Dear Mom and Dad, I am writing you this note.'

And then it stopped. When the police caught Fred-ericks he showed them the boy's body and said, 'He was such a nice boy. Why did he have to die?'

Matt Lamb – who Gary had described as not one of 'Elliott's all-stars', but almost – ended his days in less inauspicious circumstances. While whitewashing fences and pondering his future at Elliott's ranch he decided to become a soldier. The Israeli army turned him down because he was a psychopath ('See?' Gary said. 'They have standards.') But the Rhodesian army welcomed him and he died in a shoot-out with supporters of Robert Mugabe.

Most discomforting for the programme was what happened with the multiple-child-killer Peter Woodcock. This was the man Steve Smith had been attached to. He was given his first ever three-hour pass one summer's day in 1991. His psychiatrists were unaware that he had secretly pre-allotted ten minutes of it (3.10 p.m. – 3.20 p.m.) to kill a fellow psychiatric patient called Dennis Kerr who had spurned his advances. He invited Kerr into the woods behind the hospital and slashed him a hundred times.

'I did it,' he explained during his trial, 'to see what effect a hatchet would have on a body.' Kerr died as a result of 'chopping injuries' to his head and neck.

Later, after Woodcock had been returned to Oak Ridge, he was interviewed by the BBC about the murder.

INTERVIEWER: What was going through your mind at the time? This was someone you loved.

WOODCOCK: Curiosity, actually. And an anger. Because he had rebuffed all my advances.

INTERVIEWER: And why did you feel someone should die as a result of your curiosity?

WOODCOCK: I just wanted to know what it would feel like to kill somebody.

INTERVIEWER: But you'd already killed three people.

WOODCOCK: Yes but that was years and years and years and years ago.

The interview's most painful moment was when Woodcock admitted that Elliott and Gary's programme was kind of to blame, because it had taught him how to be a more devious psychopath. All those chats about empathy were like an empathy-faking finishing school for him.

'I did learn how to manipulate better,' he said, 'and keep the more outrageous feelings under wraps better.'

The Oak Ridge programme was over. Elliott Barker, crushed by the weight of evidence against his life's work, became a director of the Canadian Society for the Prevention of Cruelty to Children, specializing in counselling the children of psychopaths.

'I have certainly always felt that Elliott's heart was in the right place,' emailed a former colleague who didn't want to be named and who works at Oak Ridge today. 'He's been the subject of much criticism, of course, for his idea and methods and frequently has had malpractice suits against him. Yes, you guessed right, psychopaths from the program looking to make a lot of money.

But Bob Hare and us have always agreed that psychopaths are born that way and not created by controlling mummies and weak fathers.'

'That's lucky,' I emailed back, 'as I am a weak father and my wife is a controlling mummy.'

4

THE PSYCHOPATH TEST

'They had psychopaths *naked* and talking about their *feelings*!' Bob Hare laughed. 'They had psychopaths on *beanbags*! They had psychopaths acting as *therapists* to their fellow psychopaths!'

He shook his head at the idealism of it all.

'Incredible,' he said.

It was an August evening and I was drinking with Bob Hare in a hotel bar in rural Pembrokeshire, west Wales. He was a quite feral-looking man with yellow-white hair and red eyes, as if he'd spent his life in battle, battling psychopaths, the very forces of evil. It was exciting to finally meet him. Whilst names like Elliott Barker and Gary Maier have all but faded away, surviving only in obscure reports detailing crazily idealistic psychiatric endeavours from days long gone, Hare is influential.

Justice departments and parole boards all over the world have accepted his contention that psychopaths are quite simply incurable and everyone should concentrate their energies instead on learning how to root them out using his PCL-R Checklist, which he has spent a lifetime refining. His is not the only psychopath checklist around, but it is by far the most extensively used. It is the one used to diagnose Tony at Broadmoor and get him locked up for the past twelve years.

Bob Hare saw the Oak Ridge programme as yet more evidence of psychopaths' untrustworthiness. Teach them empathy and they'll cunningly use it as an empathy-faking training exercise for their own malicious ends. Indeed, every observer who has studied the Oak Ridge programme has come to that same conclusion. Everyone, that is, except Gary Maier.

'Yeah,' Gary told me, 'I guess we had inadvertently created a finishing school for them. There had always been that worry. But they were doing well in the program . . .'

They were doing well and then, suddenly, he got fired.

'When they saw their leader be trashed like that I think it empowered them,' Gary said. 'There was like a "This is bullshit!" And we got a rebound.'

Some of the psychopaths, Gary believed, went off and killed to teach the authorities a lesson – that's what happens when you fire a man as inspiring as Gary Maier.

He sounded mournful, defensive and utterly convinced of himself when he told me this, and I suddenly understood what a mutually passionate and sometimes dysfunctional bubble the relationship between a therapist and their client can be.

I had emailed Bob Hare to ask if he'd meet me and he'd replied that he'd be teaching his checklist to a group of psychiatrists and brain-imagers and care workers and psychologists and prison officers and budding criminal-profilers on a three-day residential course, and if I was willing to pay the £600 registration fee I was welcome to join them, although a copy of the thirty-page checklist wasn't included in the price. That would cost an extra £361.31. I negotiated his office down to £400 (media discount) and we were all set.

This was the Monday evening before the first day and the attendees were milling around. Some, clearly impressed to be in the same room as Bob Hare, approached him for his autograph. Others looked sceptical from a distance. One care worker had told me earlier that she'd been sent by her employers and she wasn't happy about it. Surely it was unfair to doom a person to a lifetime of a horrifying-sounding psychopathy diagnosis ('It's a *huge* label,' she said) just because they didn't do well on the Hare Checklist. At least in the old days it was quite simple. If someone was a persistent violent offender who lacked impulse controls they were a psychopath. But the Hare Checklist was much more wily. It was all to do with reading between the lines of a person's turn of phrase, a person's sentence construction. This was, she said, amateur-sleuth territory.

I told Bob about her scepticism and I said I shared it to an extent, but that was possibly because I'd been spending a lot of time lately with Scientologists.

He shot me a grumpy look.

'We'll see how you feel by the end of the week,' he said.

'So, anyway,' I said, 'how did all this begin for you?'

He looked at me. I could tell what was going through his mind: 'I'm tired. Telling the story will take up a lot of my energy. Does this person really deserve it?'

Then he sighed. And he began.

In the mid-1960s, just as Elliott Barker was first conceiving his Total Encounter Capsule over in Ontario, Bob Hare was in Vancouver, working as a prison psychologist. His was the maximum-security British Columbia Penitentiary. Nowadays it is a prison-themed bar and diner where the servers wear striped prison uniforms and dishes are named after famous inmates, but back then it was a tough facility with a brutal reputation. Like Elliott, Bob believed that the psychopaths in his care buried their madness beneath a facade of normality. But Bob was less idealistic. He was interested in detection, not cure. He'd been tricked so many times by devious psychopaths. On his very first day working at the prison, for example, the warden had told him he needed a uniform and he should give his measurements to the inmate who was the prison tailor. So Bob did, and was glad to observe how assiduously the man took them. He spent a long time getting everything just right: the feet, the inside leg. Bob felt moved by the sight. Even in this awful prison here was a man who took pride in his work.

But then, when the uniform arrived, Bob found that one trouser leg rode up to his calf while the other trailed along the ground. The jacket sleeves were equally askew. It couldn't have been human error. The man was obviously trying to make him look like a clown.

At every turn, psychopaths were making his life unpleasant. One even cut the brake cables of his car while it was in the prison's auto-repair shop. Bob could have been killed. And so he started devising tests to determine if psychopaths could somehow be rooted out.

He put word around the prison that he was looking for psychopathic and non-psychopathic volunteers. There was no shortage. Prisoners were always looking to relieve the boredom. He strapped them up, one by one, to various EEG and sweat- and blood-pressure-measuring machines, and also to an electricity generator, and he explained to them that he was going to count backwards from ten and when he reached one they'd receive a very painful electric shock.

The difference in the responses stunned Bob. The non-psychopathic volunteers (theirs were crimes of passion, usually, or crimes born from terrible poverty or abuse) steeled themselves ruefully, as if a painful electric shock was just the penance they deserved, and as the countdown continued the monitors revealed dramatic increases in their perspiration rates. They were, Bob noted and documented, scared.

'And what happened when you got to one?' I asked Bob.

'I gave them an electric shock,' Bob said. He smiled. 'We used *really* painful electric shocks,' he said.

'And the psychopaths?' I asked.

'They didn't break a sweat,' said Bob. 'Nothing.'

I looked at Bob.

'Sure,' he added, 'at the exact moment the unpleasant thing occurred . . .'

'The electric shock?' I asked.

'Yeah,' said Bob, 'when the unpleasant thing occurred the psychopaths gave a response . . .'

'Like a shriek?' I asked.

'Yes, I suppose like a shriek,' said Bob. But the tests seemed to indicate that the amygdala, the part of the brain that should have anticipated the unpleasantness and sent the requisite signals of fear over to the central nervous system, wasn't functioning as it should.

It was an enormous breakthrough for Bob, his first clue that the brains of psychopaths were different to regular brains. But he was even more astonished when he repeated the test. This time the psychopaths knew exactly how much pain they'd be in when he reached one, and still: nothing. No sweat. Bob learned something that Elliott Barker wouldn't for years: psychopaths were likely to reoffend.

'They had no memory of the pain of the electric shock even when the pain had occurred just moments before,' Bob said. 'So what's the point in threatening them with imprisonment if they break the terms of their parole? The threat has no meaning for them.'

He did another experiment, the Startle Reflex test, in which psychopaths and non-psychopaths were invited to look at grotesque images, like crime-scene photographs of blown-apart faces, and then when they least expected it Bob would let off an incredibly loud noise in their ear. The non-psychopaths would leap with astonishment. The psychopaths would remain comparatively serene.

Bob knew we tend to jump a lot higher when startled if we're on the edge of our seats anyway. If we're watching a scary movie and someone makes an unexpected noise we leap in terror. But if we're *engrossed* by something, a crossword puzzle, say, and someone startles us, our leap is less pronounced. From this Bob deduced that when psychopaths see grotesque images of blown-apart faces they aren't horrified. They're *absorbed*.

It seemed from Bob's experiments that psychopaths see blown-apart faces the same way we journalists see mysterious packages sent in the mail, or we see Broadmoor patients who might or might not have faked madness – as fascinating puzzles to be solved.

Thrilled by his findings, Bob sent his readings to *Science* magazine.

'The editor returned them unpublished,' he said. 'He wrote me a letter. I'll never forget it. He wrote, "Frankly we found some of the brain-wave patterns depicted in your paper very odd. Those EEGs couldn't have come from real people." '

Bob paused and chuckled.

'*Couldn't have come from real people*,' he repeated.

My guess was that *Science* magazine behaved coolly towards Bob because they believed him to be yet another maverick psychopath-researcher running rampant in a Canadian mental institution in the late 1960s. Those places were the Wild West of psychopath-study back then, with lots of big ideas and practically no regulation.

It was inevitable that civil-rights groups would eventually force a reining-in of the experiments. And sure enough, disastrously for Bob, electric shocks were outlawed in the early 1970s.

'Even mild ones,' he told me. He seemed annoyed by the legislation even now, years later. 'We could still startle them with loud noises but they couldn't be anywhere near *as* loud,' he said.

Bob was forced to change tack. How could psychopaths be rooted out in a more hands-off way? Were there patterns of behaviour? Would they involuntarily use giveaway turns of phrase, imperceptible to unsuspecting civilians? He devoured Hervey Cleckley's seminal 1941 book, *The Mask of Sanity*. Cleckley was a Georgia-based psychiatrist whose analysis of psychopathic behaviour, how they bury their psychosis beneath a veneer of engaging normalness, had come to influence the field. Bob began quietly scrutinizing his own psychopaths, looking out for linguistic clues.

In 1975 he organized a conference on the subject.

'I invited the top people in the world who might have something to say about psychopaths,' he said. 'We ended up with eighty-five people. We took over a hotel in a ski resort near St-Moritz called Les Arcs.'

It began disastrously, Bob said, with one psychiatrist standing up and dramatically announcing to the group his contention that Bob was himself a psychopath. A ripple of shock passed through the conference hall.

Bob stood. 'Why do you believe that?' he asked.

'You're clearly impulsive,' replied the psychiatrist.

'You can't plan ahead. You invited me to participate as a speaker in this conference only a month ago.'

'I invited you only a month ago because the person I wanted to come couldn't come,' Bob said.

'Oh, you're cold-blooded and callous,' the psychiatrist said.

'Did he mean it?' I asked Bob now.

'Yeah, he meant it,' said Bob. 'He was a nasty man.'

The purpose of the Les Arcs conference was for the experts to pool their observations on the minutiae of psychopaths' behaviour, the verbal and non-verbal tics. Were there patterns? Did they involuntarily use giveaway turns of phrase? Their conclusions became the basis for his now-famous twenty-point Hare PCL-R Checklist. Which was this:

ITEM 1 : Glibness/superficial charm
ITEM 2 : Grandiose sense of self-worth
ITEM 3 : Need for stimulation/proneness
            to boredom
ITEM 4 : Pathological lying
ITEM 5 : Cunning/manipulative
ITEM 6 : Lack of remorse or guilt
ITEM 7 : Shallow affect
ITEM 8 : Callous/lack of empathy
ITEM 9 : Parasitic lifestyle
ITEM 10: Poor behavioral controls
ITEM 11: Promiscuous sexual behavior
ITEM 12: Early behavior problems

ITEM 13: Lack of realistic long-term goals
ITEM 14: Impulsivity
ITEM 15: Irresponsibility
ITEM 16: Failure to accept responsibility
for own actions
ITEM 17: Many short-term marital relationships
ITEM 18: Juvenile delinquency
ITEM 19: Revocation of conditional release
ITEM 20: Criminal versatility

And first thing the next morning we were going to learn how to use it.

Tuesday morning. The attendees milled around in the marquee that was to be ours for the next three days. Some were Bob Hare fans. When he stood in a corner telling stories about how he 'pack[s] heat, because a *lot* of psychopaths blame their incarcerations on me' we gathered to listen. The peach-silk drapes fluttered in the summer morning breeze. Bob brought up the occasion – now famous in psychopath-analysing circles – when Peter Woodcock had explained that the reason why he'd killed Dennis Kerr on his first day of freedom from Oak Ridge was because he wanted to know what it would be like to kill someone, and the interviewer had said, 'But you'd already killed three people,' and Woodcock had replied, 'Yes, but that was years and years and years and years ago.'

Bob turned to me. 'You see?' he said. 'Short memories. Just like during that electric-shock test.'

• • •

Some of the people listening in chuckled wryly. But there were sceptics here too. Psychiatrists and psychologists and care workers and criminal profilers and neurologists tend not to like being told what to do by so-called gurus of the movement. I could feel in the room a sense of 'impress me'.

We took our places. Bob flicked a switch. And onto the screen came a video, of an empty room. It was drab and municipal-looking, painted in a blue so dull it was barely a colour. There was a plywood desk, a chair. The only splash of cheerfulness was a bright red button on the wall. Into the room walked a man. He was good-looking, neatly dressed. He had a bit of a twinkle in his eye. He moved his chair until it was underneath the red button. It made a slight scraping noise as he pulled it across the floor.

'Do you see what he just did?' said Bob. 'He moved his chair to right below the panic button. He did it to intimidate my researcher who's standing behind the camera. Just a little display of control. That feeling of *control* is important to them.'

And the man began to talk.

We never learned his name, nor which prison this room was situated inside. Throughout the morning we referred to him only as Case Study H. His accent was Canadian.

It all began, quite innocently, with the researcher asking Case Study H about his school days.

'I enjoyed the social atmosphere of school,' he replied, 'enjoyed learning and seeing new things.'

'Did you ever hurt anyone in a schoolyard fight?' the researcher asked.

'No,' he replied. 'Just schoolyard shenanigans.'

(These were critical questions, Bob later explained, because the answers might inform Item 12 of his checklist: *Early behavior problems*. Almost all psychopaths display serious behaviour problems as a child, Bob said, starting around age ten to twelve, like persistent bullying, vandalism, substance abuse, arson.)

'I had a couple of incidences of fisticuffs,' said Case Study H. 'Well, one time I broke this kid's arm. It was really distasteful. I was holding him down and I put excessive pressure on his arm and it just snapped. It was not something I wanted to happen.'

There was, we noted in our assessment sheets, something weirdly disconnected about his description of the event: '*I put excessive pressure on his arm and it just snapped.*' It was like he couldn't properly place himself there.

Item 7: Shallow affect – An individual who seems unable to experience a normal range and depth of emotions.

Item 8: Callous/lack of empathy.

Item 10: Poor behavioral controls.

I remembered a time I perforated my eardrum on a plane and for days afterwards everything around me seemed faraway and hazy and impossible to connect to. Was that foggy sensation a psychopath's continual emotional state?

'One of my old buds from the FBI was investigating this woman, Karla Homolka,' Bob had told me earlier. 'She and her husband had videotaped themselves torturing and raping and murdering these young women. The police were taking her through the house where they'd cut up the bodies, carved them up, and Karla was saying, "My sister would like that rug . . . " They took her into the bathroom and Karla was saying, "Can I ask you something? I had a bottle of perfume here . . . " Totally disconnected. It was stunning.'

Bob said it's always a nice surprise when a psychopath speaks openly about their inability to feel emotions. Most of them pretend to feel. When they see us non-psychopaths crying or scared or moved by human suffering, or whatever, they think it's fascinating. They study us and learn how to ape us, like space creatures trying to blend in, but if we keep our eyes open we can spot the fakery.

'What happened to Karla Homolka in the end?' I asked him.

'She's out now,' he said. 'They believed her little-girl act. Hair in braids. All sweet and lovely. Very convincing. She blamed it all on her husband. She did a plea bargain. They gave her twelve years.'

Item 5: Cunning/manipulative.

Item 4: Pathological lying – An individual for whom lying is a characteristic part of their interactions with others.

Case Study H's video testimony continued. Around the time he broke the kid's arm he locked his stepmother in a closet – revenge for her trying to discipline his brother.

Item 14: Impulsivity.

'She was in the closet for nearly twelve hours. And

then my father came home. He let her out. It was pathetic. She just sobbed.'

One time, Bob said, one of his researchers interviewed a bank robber who told him how a cashier had soiled herself from fear as he pointed his gun at her.

'It was pathetic,' the bank robber had told Bob's researcher, 'seeing her soil herself like that.'

I glanced at one or two of my fellow sceptics in the crowd. We were looking a bit less sceptical now. We took notes.

'*Item 6*,' I wrote on my pad. '*Lack of remorse or guilt.*'

'How did it feel to lock your stepmother in a closet?' the interviewer asked Case Study H.

'It felt invigorating,' he replied. 'It felt good. I had some power. I was in *control*.'

Item 2: Grandiose sense of self-worth.

'I became the night clerk at a local place,' he continued. 'If people came in drinking, swinging around, if they wouldn't respond to politeness, well then I would get physical with them. I beat a couple of people pretty bad.'

'How did you feel about that?' the interviewer asked.

'I didn't really have any feelings about it,' he replied.

We attendees glanced excitedly at each other and scribbled notes. I began thinking about the people I knew who didn't have as many feelings as they ought to have.

'Ever injure anyone badly enough to get them in to hospital?' the interviewer asked.

'I don't know,' he replied. 'I didn't care. It wasn't my problem. I won the fight. No room for second place.'

I was good at this, good at reading between the lines, at spotting the clues, the needles in the haystack. It's what I've been doing for twenty years as a journalist.

Case Study H reminded me of a blind man whose other senses had become enhanced to compensate. His enhanced qualities, compensating for the lack of guilt and fear and remorse, included the ability to skilfully manipulate – 'I was able to manipulate those people that were close to me, for drugs, for money, using my friends, the more I know about them the better I am at knowing what buttons to push,' he told Bob's researcher (*Item 9: Parasitic lifestyle*) – and also an aptitude for not feeling bad about his crimes afterwards.

'It was a business,' he shrugged, recounting one robbery he committed. 'They had insurance.'

Psychopaths, Bob said, will invariably argue that their victims had no right to complain. They had insurance. Or they learnt a valuable life lesson getting beaten up like that. Or it was their own fault anyway. One time Bob interviewed a man who had impulsively killed another man over a bar tab.

'He only had himself to blame,' the killer told Bob. 'Anybody could have seen I was in a rotten mood that night.'

Item 16: Failure to accept responsibility for own actions.

All this was building towards the moment Case Study H would detail his most awful crime. His recounting of it began quite vaguely. I didn't quite understand what he was talking about at first. There was a kid he knew. The kid hated his parents. It was a real weakness of the kid's. Case Study H thought he could get something out of this hatred. Maybe he could provoke the kid into robbing them and then they could share the money. So he started needling the kid. All his troubles were the fault of his parents. Case Study H really knew which buttons to push to rile a boy who was already on the edge.

'The more he told me about himself the more leverage I had for manipulation,' he told Bob's researcher. 'I just kept fuelling the fire, the more fuel I added to the fire the bigger payoff for me. I was the puppet master pulling the strings.'

Eventually the kid became wound so tight he got a baseball bat, jumped into his car, with Case Study H in tow, and drove to his parents' house. When they arrived, 'I sort of gave him that mocking look,' Case Study H said. ' "Show me." And he showed me. He went into the master bedroom equipped with a baseball bat and I sort of shrugged it off. And then the beatings started. It was endless. It seemed to last an eternity. He came back into the hall brandishing a baseball bat covered in blood. I came face to face with one of the victims. He didn't look real. He just didn't look real. He was looking right at me. It was just a vacant expression. There were three people in the house. One person died. The other two were severely injured.'

This was what happened when a psychopath got control of the emotions of a troubled, thuggish kid.

Bob's researcher asked him, if he could go back in

time and change things from his life what would he change?

'I have often pondered that,' Case Study H replied. 'But then all that I have learnt would be lost.' He paused. 'The hotter the fire when forging a sword the tighter the bond on the blade,' he said.

'Is there anything else you want to say?' said Bob's researcher.

'No,' he replied. 'That's it.'

'OK, thanks,' said Bob's researcher.

The video ended. We broke for lunch.

And so passed the three days. And as they did my scepticism drained away entirely and I became a Bob Hare devotee, bowled over by his discoveries. I think the other sceptics felt the same. He was very convincing. I was attaining a new power, like a secret weapon, the kind of power that heroes of TV dramas about brilliant criminal-profilers display – the power to identify a psychopath merely by spotting certain turns of phrase, certain sentence constructions, certain ways of being. I felt like a different person, a hardliner, not confused or out of my depth as I had been when I'd been hanging around with Tony and the Scientologists in Broadmoor. Instead I was contemptuous of those naive people who allowed themselves to be taken in by slick-tongued psychopaths, contemptuous of, for instance, Norman Mailer.

In 1977, Mailer – who had just published *The Executioner's Song* – began championing a tough Utah prisoner, a bank robber and murderer called Jack Abbott, whose writings he admired.

'I love Jack Abbott for surviving and for having learned to write as well as he does,' he wrote and began lobbying the Utah Board of Corrections for his release.

'Mr. Abbott has the makings of a powerful and important American writer,' he told them, promising that if they paroled him he'd give him a job as a researcher for $150 a week. Surprised, and somewhat dazzled, the Board of Corrections agreed. Jack Abbott was free. And headed straight for literary New York.

This was no surprise. New York City was where his champions were. But even so, Bob said, psychopaths tend to gravitate towards the bright lights. You'll find lots of them in New York and London and Los Angeles. A psychologist called David Cooke, of the Glasgow Centre for the Study of Violence, was once asked in Parliament if psychopaths caused particular problems in Scottish prisons.

'Not really,' he replied. 'They're all in London prisons.'

It wasn't, he told them, a throwaway line. He had spent months assessing Scottish-born prisoners for psychopathy, and the majority of those who scored high were in London, having committed their crimes there. Psychopaths get bored easily. They need excitement. They migrate to the big cities.

Item 3: Need for stimulation/proneness to boredom.

They also tend to suffer from self-delusions about their long-term prospects. They think if they move to London or New York or LA they'll make it big, as a movie star, or a great athlete, or whatever. One time one of Bob's researchers asked a grossly overweight prison psychopath what he hoped to do when he got out, and he replied that he planned to be a professional gymnast.

Item 13: Lack of realistic long-term goals.

(Unless he was joking, of course).

Jack Abbott thought he'd be the toast of literary New York. And, as it turned out, he was. He and Mailer appeared together on *Good Morning America*. He was photographed by the great New York portraitist, and wife of Kurt Vonnegut, Jill Krementz. The *New York Times* expressed gratitude to Mailer for helping get him out on parole. He signed with the powerhouse agent Scott Meredith and was guest of honour at a celebratory dinner at a Greenwich Village restaurant, where Mailer, plus the editorial directors of Random House, Scott Meredith and others toasted him with champagne.

And then, six weeks after getting out of prison, at 5.30 a.m. on 18 July 1981, Abbott stopped at a twenty-four-hour Manhattan restaurant called the Bini-Bon. He had with him (according to reports the next day) two 'attractive, well-educated young women he had met at a party'.

Item 11: Promiscuous sexual behavior.

Although, in fairness, Item 11 may not have applied to that threesome. It is impossible to know if they were all intending to have sex. Because everything was about to alter. Everything was about to get worse.

Behind the counter at the Bini-Bon was a twenty-two-year-old aspiring actor called Richard Adan. Abbott asked to use the toilet. Adan said it was for employees only. Abbott said, 'Let's go outside and settle this like men,' and so they did and Abbott got out a knife and stabbed Richard Adan to death. Then he walked away, vanishing into the night.

'What happened?' Scott Meredith said to the *New York Times*. 'Every conversation I had with Jack we talked about the future. Everything was ahead of him.'

What happened, Bob explained to us now, although we didn't need telling, was that Jack Abbott was a psychopath. He couldn't bear being disrespected. His self-worth was too grandiose for that. He couldn't control his impulses.

'When the police finally caught up with him you know what he told them about the guy he stabbed?' Bob said. 'He said, "Oh, but he would never have made it as an actor." '

'These motherfucking psychologists and psychiatrists are going to tell the administration and the police what you are going to do next. Even Jesus Christ could not predict what the fuck his apostles were going to do.'

These were the words of another of Bob's videoed case studies – Case Study J.

We laughed shrewdly when we heard him say this because we *did* now know. That cryptic, powerful knowledge of how to decipher and identify psychopaths and anticipate their next move, even when they were feigning normalcy, was ours now. What we knew was that they were remorseless monsters and they would do it again in a heartbeat.

As I sat in the marquee my mind drifted to what I could do with my new powers. If I'm being honest it didn't cross my mind at that point to become some kind of great crime fighter, an offender profiler or criminal psychologist, philanthropically dedicated to making society a safer place. Instead I made a mental list of all the people who had crossed me over the years and wondered which of them I might be able to expose as having psychopathic character traits. Top of the list of possibilities was the *Sunday Times* and *Vanity Fair* critic A. A. Gill, who had always been very rude about my television documentaries and had recently written a restaurant column in which he admitted to killing a baboon on safari.

> I took him just below the armpit. A soft-nosed .357 blew his lungs out. I wanted to get a sense of what it might be like to kill someone, a stranger. You see it in all those films: guns and bodies, barely a close-up of reflection or doubt. What does it really feel like to shoot someone, or someone's close relative?
> – A. A. Gill, *Sunday Times,* 25 October 2009

'*Item 8: Callous/lack of empathy*,' I thought.

I smiled to myself, and zoned back in to Bob. He was saying that if he were to score himself on his checklist he'd probably get a four or a five out of the possible forty. Tony in Broadmoor told me that on the three occasions they scored him, he got around a twenty-nine or a thirty.

Our three days in west Wales came to an end. On the last Bob surprised us by unexpectedly flashing onto the screen a large-scale, close-up photograph of a man who'd been shot in the face at very close range. This came after he'd lulled us into a false sense of security by flashing photographs of ducks on pretty lakes and summer days in the park. But in this picture, gore and gristle bubbled everywhere. The man's eyes had bulged all the way out of their sockets. His nose was gone.

'Oh *GOD*,' I thought.

An instant later my body responded to the shock by feeling prickly and jangly and weak and debilitated. This sensation, Bob said, was a result of our amygdalae and our central nervous systems shooting signals of distress up and down to each other. It's the feeling we get when we're suddenly startled – like when a figure jumps out at us in the dark – or when we realize we've done something terrible, the feeling of fear and guilt and remorse, the physical manifestation of our conscience.

'It is a feeling,' Bob said, 'that psychopaths are incapable of experiencing.'

Bob said it was becoming clearer that this brain anomaly is at the heart of psychopathy.

'There are all sorts of laboratory studies and the results are very, very consistent,' he said. 'What they find is that there are anomalies in the way these individuals process material that has emotional implications. That there's this dissociation between the linguistic meaning of words and the emotional connotations. Somehow they don't put them together. Various parts of the limbic system just don't light up.'

And with that our psychopath-spotting course was over. As we gathered together our belongings and headed towards our cars I said to one attendee, 'You have to feel sorry for psychopaths, right? If it's all because of their amygdalae? If it's not their fault?'

'Why should we feel sorry for them?' he replied. 'They don't give a shit about us.'

Bob Hare called over to me. He was in a hurry. He had to get the train from Cardiff to Heathrow so he could fly back to Vancouver. Could I give him a lift?

He saw it before I did. A car was upside down. The driver was still in his seat. He was just sitting there, as if good-naturedly waiting for someone to come and turn him right way up again so he could continue on his journey. I thought, 'He looks *patient*,' but then I realized he wasn't conscious.

His passenger sat on the grass a short distance away. She was sitting cross-legged, as if lost in her thoughts. She must have been thrown clean through the window a moment or two earlier.

I saw the scene only for an instant. Other people had already parked their cars and were running towards them, so I kept going, pleased that I didn't have to be the one to handle it. Then I wondered if I should worry that my relief at not having to deal with the unpleasant responsibility was a manifestation of *Item 8: Callous/lack of empathy* – '*He is only concerned with Number 1*'.

I glanced in my rear-view mirror at the good Samaritans rushing over and surrounding the overturned car and continued on my way.

'Jon?' said Bob, after a moment.

'Mm?' I said.

'Your driving,' said Bob.

'What about my driving?' I said.

'You're swerving all over the road,' said Bob.

'No I'm not,' I said. We continued in silence for a moment. 'It's the shock of seeing the crash,' I said.

It was good to know that I had been affected after all.

Bob said what was happening was my amygdala and central nervous system were shooting signals of fear and distress up and down to each other.

'They certainly are,' I nodded. 'I can actually feel it happening. It's very jarring and jaggedy.'

'You do realize,' said Bob, 'that psychopaths would see that crash and their amygdalae would barely register a thing.'

'Well, then, I'm the opposite of a psychopath,' I said. 'If anything my amygdala and my central nervous system shoot far too many signals up and down to each other.'

'Can you concentrate on the road, please,' said Bob.

'I came to you,' I said, 'because of this guy called Tony. He's in Broadmoor. He says they're falsely accusing him of psychopathy and he hopes I'll do some campaigning journalism to support his release. And I do have warm feelings for Tony, I really do, but how do I know if he's a psychopath . . . ?'

Bob didn't seem to be listening. It was as if the crash had made him introspective. He said, almost to himself, 'I shouldn't have done my research just in prisons. I should have spent some time inside the Stock Exchange as well.'

I looked at Bob. 'Really?' I said.

He nodded.

'But surely stock-market psychopaths can't be as bad as serial-killer psychopaths,' I said.

'Serial killers ruin families,' shrugged Bob. 'Corporate and political and religious psychopaths ruin economies. They ruin societies.'

This – Bob was saying – was the straightforward solution to the greatest mystery of all: why is the world so unfair? Why all that savage economic injustice, those brutal wars, the everyday corporate cruelty? The answer: psychopaths. That part of the brain that doesn't function right. You're standing on an escalator and you watch the people going past on the opposite escalator. If you could climb inside their brains you would see we aren't all the same. We aren't all good people just trying to do good. Some of us are *psychopaths*. And psychopaths are to blame for this brutal, misshapen society. They're the rocks thrown into the still pond.

It wasn't only Bob who believed that a disproportionate number of psychopaths can be found in high places. In the days after Essi Viding had first mentioned the theory to me I spoke to scores of psychologists who all said exactly the same. One was Martha Stout from the Harvard Medical School and author of *The Sociopath Next Door*. (You may be wondering what the difference is between a psychopath and a sociopath, and the answer is, there really isn't one. Psychologists and psychiatrists around the world tend to use the terms interchangeably.) They are everywhere, she said. They are in the crowded restaurant where you have your lunch. They are in your open-plan office.

'As a group they tend to be more charming than most people,' she said. 'They have no warm emotions of their own but will study the rest of us. They're the boss or the co-worker who likes to make other people jump just for the pleasure of seeing them jump. They're the spouse who marries to look socially normal but inside the marriage shows no love after the initial charm wears off.'

'I don't know how many people will read this book,' I said to her. 'Maybe a hundred thousand? So that means around a thousand of them will be psychopaths. Possibly even more if psychopaths like reading books about psychopaths. What should my message to them be? Turn yourselves in?'

'That would be nice,' Martha said. 'But their arrogance would hold up. They'd think, "She's lying about there being conscience." Or "This poor dear is restrained by conscience. She should be more like me." '

'What if the wife of a psychopath reads this?' I asked. 'What should she do? Leave?'

'Yes,' said Martha. 'I would like to say leave. You're not going to hurt someone's feeling because there are no feelings to hurt.' She paused. 'Sociopaths love power. They love winning. If you take loving kindness out of the human brain there's not much left except the will to win.'

'Which means you'll find a preponderance of them at the top of the tree?' I said.

'Yes,' she said. 'The higher you go up the ladder the greater the number of sociopaths you'll find there.'

'So the wars, the injustices, the exploitation, all of these things occur because of that tiny per cent of the population up there who are mad in this certain way?' I asked. It sounded like the ripple effect of Petter Nordland's book, but on a giant scale.

'I think a lot of these things are initiated by them,' she said.

'It is a frightening and huge thought,' I said, 'that the ninety-nine per cent of us wandering around down here are having our lives pushed and pulled around by that psychopathic fraction up there.'

'It is a large thought,' she said. 'It is a thought people don't have very often. Because we're raised to believe that deep down everyone has conscience.'

At the end of our conversation she turned to address you, the reader. She said, if you're beginning to feel worried that you may be a psychopath, if you recognize some of those traits in yourself, if you're feeling a creeping anxiety about it, that means you are not one.

Everyone in the field seemed to regard psychopaths in this same way: inhuman, relentlessly wicked forces, whirlwinds of malevolence, forever harming society but impossible to identify unless you're trained in the subtle art of spotting them, as I now was. The only other way would be to have access to some expensive fMRI equipment, like Adam Perkins does.

Adam is a research fellow in clinical neuroscience at the Institute of Psychiatry, South London. I had visited him shortly after meeting Essi because he's an expert in anxiety, and I wanted to test out my theory on him that suffering from anxiety is the neurological opposite of being a psychopath when it comes to amygdala function. I imagined my amygdala to be like one of those Hubble photographs of a solar storm, and I imagined psychopaths' amygdalae to be like those Hubble photographs of dead planets, like Pluto. Adam verified my theory, and then to demonstrate he strapped me up to some wires, put me into a dummy fMRI scanner, and without any warning gave me a very painful electric shock.

'Ow!' I yelled. 'That really hurts. Would you please turn down the level of the electric shock? I mean, I thought that had been outlawed. What was that level?'

'Three,' said Adam.

'What does it go up to?' I asked.

'Eight,' he said.

Adam performed various tests on me to monitor my anxiety level, and for much of it I glared suspiciously at the button that administered the electric shock, sometimes letting off little involuntary spasms, and when it was over he confirmed from his EEG readings that I was indeed above average on the anxiety scale.

'Ooh!' I thought, unexpectedly pleased to hear that there really was something identifiably wrong with me. Then I said, 'I suppose it probably isn't a great idea for a man like me who suffers from excessive anxiety to chase after people who have a pathological deficit of anxiety.'

Adam nodded. He said I really had to be careful. Psychopaths are truly dangerous, he said. And they're often the people you least expect them to be.

'When I was doing my Ph.D.,' he said, 'I devised this personality test, and I advertised for volunteers amongst the student population, I put notices on the noticeboard, and a girl turned up. Young girl. She was a second-year student. About nineteen. She said, "This is a personality test, isn't it?" I said, "Yes." She said, "I've got a *bad* personality. I like to hurt people." I thought she was winding me up. I said, "OK, fine." So we went through the tests. When she was looking at the photographs of the mutilated bodies the sensors showed that she was getting a kick off of them. Her sexual-reward centre – it's a sexual thing – was fired up by blood and death. It's subconscious. It happens in milliseconds. She found those things *pleasant*.'

I looked over at Adam. Describing the moment was obviously making him feel uncomfortable. He was an anxious man, like me, hence, he said, his decision to dedicate his life to the study of the relationship between anxiety and the brain.

'She told me she'd tried to join the RAF,' he said, 'because they're the only part of the Ministry of Defence that allow women to operate weapons systems, but they sussed her out and rejected her. So she ended up doing history. Hers wasn't psychopathy in terms of being a manipulative conman. She told me about her homicidal desire the minute she met me, which suggests she wouldn't score high on the trait of smooth deceptiveness. But at the core of psychopathy is a lack of moral restraint. If a person lacks moral restraint and also happens to get turned on by violence then you end up with a very dangerous serial-killer type who lusts after killing and doesn't have any moral hang-ups about doing so. There must be people in the population who get turned on by killing but have moral restraints that prevent them from acting out their fantasies, unless they're drunk or tired or whatever. I guess she falls into this category, which is why she tried to join the RAF, so she could obtain a socially respectable opportunity to gratify her homicidal urges.'

'So what did you *do* about her?' I asked. 'Did you call the police?'

'I was put in a difficult position,' he said. 'She hadn't done any crimes. My hands were tied. There are no mechanisms in place to stop her.'

Adam and Bob and Martha seemed sure that with psychopaths, chaos was a foregone conclusion. This girl, forbidden from killing in a socially acceptable way, will probably end up as 'one of those angel of death nurses or something', Adam said. Someone who just *has* to murder.

I wondered if it ever crossed Adam's and Bob's minds that the logical solution to the psychopath problem would be to lock them up before they'd actually done anything wrong – even if proposing such a measure would make them the villains from an Orwell novel, which isn't something anyone imagines they'll be when setting out on their career path.

'Where is this woman now?' I asked Adam. 'Maybe I could meet her for my book? In a busy cafe or something.'

'I've no means of tracking her down,' Adam said.

'Participants in my studies are recorded only by numbers, not by name.' He fell silent for a second. 'So she's gone,' he said.

Adam's point was that now I was in the psychopath-spotting business I should be very vigilant. This was a perilous game. I had to trust nobody. These people were unsafe to be around. And sometimes psychopaths were nineteen-year-old women studying history in a London university.

'They come in all shapes and sizes,' he said.

Now, as Bob Hare and I neared Cardiff, I considered his theory about psychopathic CEOs and psychopathic politicians and I remembered Items 18 and 12 on his checklist – *Juvenile delinquency* and *Early behavior problems* – '*An individual who has a history of serious antisocial behavior*'.

'If some political or business leader had a psychopathically hoodlum childhood wouldn't it come out in the press and ruin them?' I said.

'They find ways to bury it,' Bob replied. 'Anyway, early behavioral problems doesn't necessarily mean ending up in Juvenile Hall. It could mean, say, secretly torturing animals.' He paused. 'But getting access to people like that can be difficult. Prisoners are easy. They like meeting researchers. It breaks up the monotony of their day. But CEOs, politicians . . .' Bob looked at me. 'It's a really big story,' he said. 'It's a story that could change forever the way people see the world . . .'

Suddenly Tony in Broadmoor felt a long way away. Bob was right: this really could be a big story. And my desire to unearth it outweighed any anxieties that were bubbling up inside me. I had to journey, armed with my new psychopath-spotting abilities, into the corridors of power.

5

TOTO

Somewhere in a long, flat expanse of nothingness between Woodstock and Albany, upstate New York, sits
a forbidding Victorian-looking building with concrete
and barbed-wire tentacles snaking out across the empty
fields. It's called the Coxsackie Correctional Facility.
Although it was mid-May sheets of icy rain bombard-
ed me as I wandered around the perimeter, not knowing
what to do. Back when I visited Broadmoor letters of
confirmation had arrived weeks earlier, lists of visiting
hours and detailed regulations. Here there was nothing.
No signs, no guards. On the phone a distant, crackly
voice had told me to 'yeahjustcomewhenever'. This place
was truly the Wild West, visitor-procedure-wise. It was
confusing, unordered, and unnerving.

There was only one person on the landscape: a young
woman shivering in a glass shelter, so I went and stood
near her.

'It's cold,' I said.

'It's always cold here,' she said.

Eventually, we heard a clang. A gate automatically opened, and we walked through an outdoor metal corridor underneath a tapestry of barbed wire and into a dark lobby filled with prison guards.

'Hello,' I said, cheerfully.

'Hey, well look who it is!' hollered one. 'Harry Potter.'

The guards surrounded me.

'Hello mister jolly old mister marvellous,' someone said.

'Oh, ribbing!' I said.

'Jolly good jolly good,' they said. 'Who are you here to see?'

'Emmanuel Constant,' I said.

At this, they stopped laughing.

'He's a mass-murderer,' said a guard, looking quite impressed.

'He once had dinner with Bill Clinton,' said another. 'Have you met him before?'

1997. Emmanuel 'Toto' Constant stood on the sidewalk of a long, flat, residential street in Queens, New York, looking up and down, trying to spot me. Far away in the distance, through the heat haze and the traffic fumes, you could just make out the Manhattan skyline, a glint of the Chrysler Building, the Twin Towers, but there were no magnificent skyscrapers around here, no downtown bars full of sophisticates, just boxy one-storey video-rental places and fast-food restaurants. Unlike his neighbours, who were dressed in T-shirts and shorts and baseball caps on this hot day, Toto Constant was wearing an immaculate pale suit with a silk handkerchief in his top pocket. He was manicured and dapper (very similarly dapper, in retrospect, to how I would first see Tony, years later, in Broadmoor).

I pulled up and parked.

'Welcome to Queens,' he said, sounding apologetic.

There was a time, in the early 1990s, when Toto Constant owned a sprawling art-deco mansion with a swimming pool and fountains in Port-au-Prince, Haiti. He was skinny and handsome and charismatic and was seen around town carrying an Uzi or a .357 magnum. It was from his mansion he set up a far-right paramilitary group, FRAPH, created to terrorize supporters of the recently exiled left-wing democratic President Jean-Bertrand Aristide. It was unclear back then who was backing Constant, who was paying his way.

According to human rights groups like the Center for Constitutional Rights and Human Rights Watch, when FRAPH caught an Aristide supporter they'd sometimes slice off their face. When a group of Aristide supporters holed up in a shanty town called Cité Soleil, Constant's men turned up with gasoline – this was December, 1993 – and burned the place to the ground. At one point that day some children tried to run away from the fire. The men from FRAPH caught them and forced them back inside their burning homes. There were fifty murders that day, and many other bloodbaths during Constant's reign. In April 1994, for example, FRAPH men raided a harbour town called Raboteau, another centre of Aristide support. They arrested and beat and shot and dunked into the open sewers all the residents they could catch. They commandeered fishing boats so they could shoot people fleeing across the sea.

> The modus operandi of FRAPH was to team up with members of the Haitian Armed Forces in midnight raids of the poorest neighborhoods of Port-au-Prince, Gonaives and other cities. In a typical raid, the attackers would invade a house in search of evidence of pro-democracy activity, such as photos of Aristide. The men of the house would frequently be abducted and subjected to torture; many would be summarily executed. The women would frequently be gang-raped, often in front of the remaining family members. The ages of documented victims range from as young as 10 to as old as 80. According to witness reports, sons were forced at gunpoint to rape their own mothers.
>
> – The Centre for Justice and Accountability

Aristide was restored to power in October 1994 and Toto Constant fled to America, leaving photos of the mutilated bodies of FRAPH victims pasted to the walls of his Port-au-Prince headquarters. He was arrested in New York. US authorities announced their intention to deport him back to Port-au-Prince so he could stand trial for crimes against humanity. There was much celebrating in Haiti. In readiness for the impending trial three women stepped forward to tell prosecutors they had been raped by Constant's men and left for dead. His fate looked sealed.

But he had one play left. From his jail cell he announced on CBS's *60 Minutes* that he was ready to reveal the names of his backers, the mysterious men who had encouraged the creation of FRAPH and put him on their payroll. They were agents from the CIA and the Defense Intelligence Agency.

'If I'm guilty of the crimes they say I was,' he told the interviewer, Ed Bradley, 'the CIA is also guilty.'

It wasn't easy to understand why the CIA would want to back a murderous, anti-democratic death squad. Aristide was a charismatic man, a leftist, a former priest. Maybe they feared he was a Castro in the making, a man who might threaten business relations between Haiti and the US.

Still, if anyone doubted Constant's word, they didn't for long. He implied that should the extradition go ahead, he'd reveal devastating secrets about American foreign policy in Haiti. Almost immediately – on 14 June 1996 – the US authorities released him from jail and gave him a green card to work in the US. But there were conditions, laid out in a five-page settlement deal that was faxed by the US Department of Justice to the prison's booking area and handed to Constant on his exit. He was forbidden from ever talking to the media.

He had to move in with his mother in Queens and could never, ever leave the borough, except for an hour each week when he was to check in with the INS (the United States Immigration and Naturalization Service) in Manhattan. But as soon as he checked in he had to drive straight back to Queens.

Queens was to be his prison.

When I heard this story back in the late 1990s I decided to approach Toto Constant for an interview. I wanted to learn how a man used to wielding such tremendous, malevolent power was adapting to life back home in the suburbs with his mother. Now he had crash-landed into the ordinary world, would the memory of his crimes eat him up, like Dostoyevsky's Raskolnikov? Plus, Queens had a thriving Haitian community, which meant he was surely living amongst some of his victims. I wrote to him, fully expecting a refusal. Talking to me would, after all, have violated the terms of his release. If the authorities found out he could be arrested, deported back to Haiti and executed. Prospective interviewees tend to turn me down for a lot less than that. Many decline my interview requests simply because they think I might portray them as a little crazy. Nonetheless, he cheerfully agreed to meet me. I didn't ask why because I was just glad to get the interview and – if I'm honest – I didn't really worry about what would happen to him as a result, which I suppose is a little *Item 6: Lack of remorse or guilt*, *Item 7: Shallow affect*, and *Item 8: Callous/ lack of empathy*, but he was a death-squad leader, so who cares?

That day in Queens was a strange and memorable one. Well-dressed men came and went. They sometimes huddled in corners and talked about things I couldn't hear, although I strained to eavesdrop. Maybe they were planning a military coup.

I asked him how he was adjusting to everyday life. What did he do to pass the time? Did he have hobbies? He smiled slightly.

'I'll show you,' he said.

He led me from his mother's house and down an alleyway, and then down another alleyway, and into a cluster of apartment blocks.

'Nearly there,' he said. 'Don't worry!'

We climbed the stairs. I looked apprehensively behind me. We reached a doorway. He opened it. I took in the room.

On every table, every surface, there were the kinds of tiny plastic figures that come free with McDonald's and Burger King promotions – little Dumbos and Goofys and Muppets from Space and Rugrats and Batmen and Powerpuff Girls and Men in Black and Luke Skywalkers and Bart Simpsons and Fred Flintstones and Jackie Chans and Buzz Lightyears and on and on.

We looked at each other.

'What impresses me most about them is the artistry,' he said.

'Do you arrange them into battalions?' I asked.

'No,' he said.

There was a silence.

'Shall we go?' he murmured, I think regretting his decision to show me his army of plastic cartoon figurines.

A few minutes later we were back in his mother's house, the two of us sitting at the kitchen table. His mother shuffled in and out. He was telling me that one day the people of Haiti would call him back to lead them – 'They adore me in Haiti,' he said – and, yes, when that day came he would do his duty for the people.

I asked him about Cité Soleil and Raboteau and the other charges against him.

'There's not even *smoke* to those claims,' he said. 'Not even *smoke*!'

'Is that it?' I thought. 'Is that all you're going to say on the subject?'

'The lies they tell about me break my heart,' he said.

And then I heard a strange noise coming from Constant. His body was shaking. The noise I could hear was something like sobbing. But it wasn't quite sobbing. It was an approximation of sobbing. His face was screwed up like a face would be if it were crying, but it was weird, like bad acting. A grown man in a dapper suit was pretending to cry in front of me. This would have been awkward enough if he was *actually* crying – I find displays of overt emotion not at all pleasant – but this was a man palpably simulating crying, which made the moment at once awkward, surreal and quite disturbing.

Our time together ended soon afterwards. He showed me to his door, the epitome of good manners, laughing, giving me a warm handshake, saying we'd meet again soon. Just as I reached my car I turned around to wave again, and when I saw him I felt a jolt pass through me – like my amygdala had just shot a signal of fear through to my central nervous system. His face was very different, much colder, suspicious. He was scrutinizing me hard. The instant I caught his eye he put on that warm look again. He grinned and waved. I waved back, climbed into the car, and drove away.

I never wrote up my interview with Toto Constant. There was something eerily vacant about him. I couldn't find a way in. But throughout my time in west Wales I kept recalling images from our day together. That fake crying seemed very *Item 7: Shallow affect – 'Displays of emotion are dramatic, shallow, short lived, leaving the impression that he is play acting'* and also extremely *Item 16: Failure to accept responsibility for own actions*. The assertion about the people of Haiti adoring him struck me as somewhat *Item 2: Grandiose sense of self-worth – 'He may claim that others respect him, fear him, envy him, dislike him, and so forth'*. His belief that he would one day return to Haiti as their leader seemed quite *Item 13: Lack of realistic long-term goals*. Maybe Bob's checklist even solved the mystery of why he agreed to meet me at all. Maybe it was *Item 3: Need for stimulation/proneness to boredom* and *Item 14: Impulsivity – 'He is unlikely to spend much time considering the possible consequences of his actions'*, as well as *Item 2: Grandiose sense of self-worth*.

Maybe *Items 3, 14* and *2* are the reasons why loads of my interviewees agree to meet me.

I couldn't see where the collection of Burger King figurines fitted in but I supposed there was no reason why psychopaths shouldn't have unrelated hobbies.

Where was he now? After I returned from Wales I did a search. He was, unexpectedly, housed in the Coxsackie Correctional Facility, two years into a twelve-to-thirty-seven-year sentence for mortgage fraud.

Item 20: Criminal versatility.

I wrote to him. I reminded him of our last meeting, gave him a potted account of amygdala dysfunction, asked him if he felt it applied to him. He wrote back that I was welcome to pay him a visit. I booked a flight. The Icelandic volcano erupted. I booked another flight a week later, and now here I was, sitting at a table marked Row 2 Table 6 in an almost empty visitors' room.

Coxsackie had one thousand prisoners. Only four had company today. There was a young couple playing cards, an elderly inmate surrounded by his children and grandchildren, the woman I'd met in the shelter, holding an inmate's hand across the table, casually snaking her fingers through his, pulling at each finger, touching his face, and Toto Constant, sitting opposite me.

He had been led here five minutes earlier and I was already struck by what easy company he was proving to be. He was doing what I expected he would, protesting his innocence of the mortgage fraud, saying he was guilty only of 'trusting the wrong people', expressing shock at the gigantic sentence, mortgage fraud usually only getting you five years.

'Five years,' he said. 'Fine. OK. But *thirty-seven years*?'

It was true that the length of the sentence didn't seem fair, in a way. I empathized with him a little about this. I told him, with some nervousness, that the brain anomaly I spoke of in my letter would, if he had it, classify him as a psychopath.

'Well, I'm not one,' he said.

'Would you be happy to explore the issues with me anyway?' I said.

'Sure,' he said. 'Fire away.'

I figured we both had something to gain from the meeting. He was a bit of a guinea pig for me, I could practise my psychopath-spotting skills on him, and he'd have a day out of his cell, away from the monotony, eating burgers bought by me from the machine in the corner of the visitors' room.

What did I hope to accomplish? I wondered if I'd catch a glimpse of Tony in Toto – maybe I'd identify some shared personality traits, just as Bob's course had taught me – and I had a bigger objective too. Terrible things had been done in Haiti in his name. He had profoundly altered Haitian society for three years, sent it spiralling frantically in the wrong direction, destroying the lives of thousands, tainting hundreds of thousands more. Was Bob Hare and Martha Stout's theory right? Was it all because of some malfunctioning relationship between his amygdala and his central nervous system? If so it was a powerful brain anomaly indeed.

'Why didn't you come and see me last Tuesday?' he asked me.

'That volcano erupted in Iceland and everything got put on hold,' I said.

'Ah!' he said, nodding. 'OK. I understand. When I got your letter I was so excited!'

'Really?' I said.

'All the inmates were saying, "The guy who wrote the *Men Who Stare At Goats* book is coming to visit YOU? Wow!" Ha ha! Everyone in here has heard of that movie!'

'Really!' I said.

'Yeah, we have a movie night every Saturday night. Last Saturday was *Avatar*. That movie touched me. It *touched* me. The invasion of the small nation by the big nation. I found those blue people beautiful. I found a beauty in them.'

'Are you an emotional man?' I asked.

'I am emotional,' he nodded. 'Anyway, a couple of months ago they chose the *Men Who Stare At Goats* movie. Most of the inmates didn't know what the hell was going on. They were saying, "What's *this*?" But I was saying, "No no, I've met the guy who wrote the book! You don't understand the guy's mind!" And then you wrote to me and said you wanted to meet me again. Everyone was so *jealous*.'

'Oh! That's nice!' I said.

'When I heard you were coming last week my hair was a real mess but I wasn't scheduled to have my hair cut so another inmate said, "You take my slot." We switched slots at the barber shop! And someone else gave me a brand-new green shirt to wear!'

'Oh *God*!' I said.

He waved his hand to say, 'I know it's silly.' 'The only

little thing we have here is a visit,' he explained. 'It's the only little thing we have left.' He fell silent. 'I once ate in the most beautiful restaurants in the world. Now I'm in a cell. I dress in green all the time.'

'Who is the unfeeling one?' I thought. I only came here to hone my psychopath-spotting skills and this poor guy borrowed a *special shirt*.

'Some guys here won't accept visitors because of what we have to go through afterwards,' said Toto.

'What do you have to go through afterwards?' I asked.

'A strip search,' he said.

'Oh *God*!' I said.

He shuddered.

'The indignity of it is awful,' he said.

Just then I looked up. Something had changed in the room. Prisoners and their loved ones were bristling, anxiously, noticing something I hadn't noticed.

'This is fucked up,' Toto whispered.

'What is?'

'That guy.'

Without taking his eyes off me Toto indicated a prison guard – a man wearing a white shirt – who was wandering the room.

'He's a sadist,' he said. 'When he walks into a room, everyone gets scared. None of us want trouble. We all just want to go home.'

'Did he just do something?'

'Not really. He told a woman that her T-shirt was too revealing. That's all.'

I glanced over. It was the woman I had met in the shelter. She was looking upset.

'It's just . . . he scares people,' he said.

'All those years ago, when I met you, something happened,' I said. 'It was right at the end of the day. I was heading to my car and I turned around and saw you staring at me. Really observing me. I saw you do the same thing when you walked into this room. You scanned the place, observing everything.'

'Yes, observing people is one of my biggest assets,' he said. 'I always observe.'

'Why?' I asked. 'What are you looking for?'

There was a short silence. Then Toto softly said, 'I want to see if people like me.'

'If people *like* you?' I said.

'I want people to think I'm a gentleman,' he said. 'I want people to like me. If people don't like me it hurts me. It's important for me to be liked. I'm sensitive to people's reactions to me. I'm observing people to see if they really like me.'

'Wow,' I said. 'I never thought you'd care so much about whether people *like* you.'

'I do.'

'That's really surprising,' I said.

I scowled inwardly. I had driven all this way and there was nothing psychopathic about him at all. He was self-effacing, humble, emotional, self-deprecating, strangely diminutive for such a large man. True, there had been admissions – a few moments earlier – of *Item 11: Promiscuous sexual behavior*, but that struck me as a rather puritanical addition to the checklist anyway.

'I'm a ladies' man,' he'd said. 'I always had a lot of women. Apparently I'm good company.' He shrugged, modestly.

'How many children do you have?'

'Seven.'

'With how many mothers?'

'Almost as many!' he laughed.

'Why so many women?'

'I don't know.' He looked genuinely perplexed. 'I've always wanted lots of women. I don't know why.'

'Why not stick with one woman?'

'I don't know. Maybe it is because I really want people to like me. So I learn how to please people. I never disagree with anyone. I make them feel good so they like me.'

'Isn't that a weakness?' I finally said. 'Your desperate desire to have people like you. Isn't that a weakness?'

'Ah no!' Toto laughed. He animatedly waved his finger at me. 'It's not a weakness at all!'

'Why?' I asked.

'I'll *tell* you why!' He smiled, winked conspiratorially, and said: 'If people like you, you can manipulate them to do whatever you want them to do!'

I blinked.

'So you don't *really* want people to like you?' I asked.

'Oh no,' he shrugged. 'I'm giving you my deepest secrets here, Jon!'

'When you said, "If people don't like me it hurts me," you don't mean it hurts your feelings. You mean it hurts your status?'

'Yes, exactly.'

'How does it work?' I asked. 'How do you make people like you?'

'Ah, OK,' he said. ' Watch this . . .'

He turned to the elderly inmate whose children and grandchildren had just left.

'You have a lovely family!' he called to him.

The man's face broke into a broad, grateful smile. 'Thanks!' he called back.

Toto grinned covertly at me.

'What about empathy?' I asked. 'Do you feel empathy? I suppose empathy could sometimes be considered a weakness.'

'No,' said Toto. 'I don't feel empathy.' He shook his head like a horse with a fly on its nose. 'It's not a feeling I have. It's not an emotion I have. Feeling sorry for people?'

'Yes.'

'I don't feel sorry for people. No.'

'What about emotions?' I said. 'You said earlier that you were an emotional person. But feeling emotions might be considered, um, a weakness.'

'Ah, but you *select* the kind of emotion you want,' he replied. 'You see? I'm really telling you my deepest secrets, Jon.'

'How about those three women who testified against you in court?' I asked. 'Do you feel any emotions at all about them?'

Toto exhaled, crossly. 'Three ladies said masked, un-identified men tortured and raped them and left them for dead and blah blah blah.' He scowled. 'They assumed they were FRAPH members because they were wearing FRAPH uniforms. They say I raped for power.'

'What did they say happened to them?'

'Oh,' he airily replied, 'one said they beat her, raped her, left her for dead. A "doctor" – when he said 'doctor' he did that dismissive quotation-mark thing with his fingers – 'said one of the attackers got her pregnant.'

He said none of the accusations were true – not a single one – and if I wanted to know more about the untruths I should wait to read his thus far half-completed memoir, *Echoes of my Silence*.

I asked Toto if he liked the other inmates and he said not really. Certainly not those who 'whine or complain. And thieves. Call me a murderer or an assassin but don't call me a thief. Also I don't like people who are lazy. Or weak. Or liars. I hate liars.'

He said his behavioural controls were nonetheless unimpeachable. Often he'd like to punch a fellow inmate's lights out, but he never did. Like just yesterday in the canteen. An inmate was slurping his soup – 'slurp slurp slurp, oh my God, Jon, it was getting on my nerves. Slurp. Slurp. Slurp. Oh I felt like punching him, but I thought, "No, Emmanuel. Wait it out. The moment will be over soon. And it was." ' Toto looked at me. 'I am wasting my time in here, Jon. That's the worst thought of all. I am wasting my time.'

Our three hours were up. On my way out the guards asked me why I'd come to visit Toto Constant and I said, 'I wanted to find out if he's a psychopath.'

'Nah, he's not a psychopath,' replied two of them, in unison.

'Hey,' said another. 'Did you know he once had dinner with Bill Clinton?'

'I don't think he ever did have dinner with Bill Clinton,' I replied. 'If he told you that I'm not sure it's true.'

The guard didn't say anything.

As I drove back to New York City I congratulated myself on being a genius, on cracking him open. The key had been the word 'weakness'. Whenever I'd said it he'd felt the necessity to reveal his hardness.

I was surprised at how easily I'd surrendered to him until then. He had presented me with a little self-effacing charm and I'd instantly labelled him a non-psychopath. There had been something reassuringly familiar about him at the beginning. He'd seemed diminutive, self-deprecating, nebbishy, which are all the things I am. Could he have been mirroring me, reflecting myself back at me? Could that be why partners of psychopaths sometimes stay in bewildering relationships?

Bob Hare said psychopaths were skilful imitators. He once told a journalist a story about how he'd been asked to consult on a Nicole Kidman movie called *Malice*. She wanted to prepare for a role as a psychopath. Bob told her, 'Here's a scene you can use. You're walking down a street and there's an accident. A car has hit a child. A crowd of people gather round. You walk up, the child's lying on the ground and there's blood running all over the place. You get a little blood on your shoes and you look down and say, "Oh shit." You look over at the child, kind of interested, but you're not repelled or horrified. You're just interested. Then you look at the mother, and you're really fascinated by the mother, who's emoting, crying out, doing all these different things. After a few minutes you turn away and go back to your house. You go into the bathroom and practise mimicking the facial expressions of the mother. That's the psychopath: somebody who doesn't understand what's going on emotionally, but understands that something important has happened.'

But Toto Constant was engagingly enigmatic too, a quality that flourishes in absence. We are dazzled by people who withhold something, and psychopaths always do because they are not all there. They are surely the most enigmatic of all the mentally disordered.

The drive from Coxsackie to New York, past Saugerties and New Paltz and Poughkeepsie, was flat and bleak – like an alien planet from a *Star Trek* episode – and I suddenly felt incredibly paranoid that Toto might turn against me and ask one of his brothers or uncles to come after me. I felt lashed by anxiety, like the sleet that was lashing the car, and so I spun it off the road and into a drive-in Starbucks that happened to be right there.

I pulled out my notes – I'd scribbled them on hotel notepaper with a prison-issue pencil – and read the part where he'd told me he was all alone in the world, that his family and everyone who had ever loved him had abandoned him.

'Oh, well, that's OK then,' I thought. The realization that his brothers and uncles had deserted him and were therefore not likely to track me down and retaliate made me feel a lot less anxious.

'I suppose that is a bit *Item 8: Callous/lack of empathy*,' I thought. 'But under the circumstances I don't care.'

I bought an americano, jumped back in the car, and carried on driving.

I supposed it shouldn't be a surprise to discover that the head of a death squad would score high on Bob Hare's psychopathic checklist. I was more interested by Bob's theory about corporate psychopaths. He blamed psychopaths for the brutal excesses of capitalism itself, that the system at its cruellest was a manifestation of a few people's anomalous amygdalae. He had written a book about it – *Snakes in Suits: When Psychopaths Go To Work* – co-authored with a psychologist named Paul Babiak. Human Resources magazines across the world had, on its publication, given it rave reviews.

'All managers and HR people should read this book,' read a typical one from *Health Service Journal*, the in-house magazine for the National Health Service. 'Do you work with a snake on the make? These people can be found among those impressive but ruthless types who cut a swathe to the jobs at the top.'

All that talk of snakes adopting human form reminded me of a story I once did about a conspiracy theorist named David Icke who believed that the secret rulers of the world were giant blood-drinking child-sacrificing lizards who had shape-shifted into humans so they could perform their evil on an unsuspecting population. I suddenly realized how similar the two stories were, except in this one the people who spoke of snakes in suits were eminent and utterly sane psychologists, respected around the world. Was this a conspiracy theory that was actually true?

As I approached New York City, the skyscrapers of the financial district growing larger, I wondered: might there be some way of proving it?

6

NIGHT OF THE
LIVING DEAD

Shubuta, Mississippi, is a dying town. Sarah's House of Glamour (a beauty salon), the Jones Brothers Market Basket Meats and Groceries Store, the Bank of Shubuta, all boarded up, alongside other storefronts so faded you can't even make out what they once were. The odd teddy bear or inflatable Santa peering through a dusty window display offers some clues to the abandoned business. Even the Shubuta Masonic Lodge is overgrown and rotting. So much for the power they thought they wielded! It didn't save them.

The jail is gone too, its iron cages crumbling and corroding inside a stone building just off Main Street, near a decaying basketball hoop.

'You know you're in a depressed place when even the jail has shut down,' I said.

'Depressed is right,' said Brad, the local man who was showing me around.

Decomposing timber protruded violently from abandoned homes like that photograph of the blown-apart face Bob Hare showed us back in the marquee in west Wales, with his gore and gristle bubbling through what remained of his skin.

Shubuta was not empty. A few remaining residents still wandered up and down. Some were drunk. Some were very old.

• • •

Shubuta had once been a thriving place.

'Bustling!' said Brad. 'Every day! Unbelievable! It was always real busy. It was wonderful growing up here. Crime was low.'

'We rode our bicycles everywhere we wanted to go,' added Brad's friend Libby. 'We rode on roller skates. Our mothers never worried about us.'

'Everyone worked up at Sunbeam,' said Brad.

Sunbeam, the local plant, made toasters. They were beautiful, art-deco looking things.

Sunbeam toasters.

Brad and I climbed over rubble and into a long building in the middle of Main Street. Its door hung from its hinges. The exit sign lay in the dust on the ground. Torn-off strands of what looked to have been red velvet curtains hung limply from masonry nails, like a scene from an abattoir.

'What did this place used to be?' I asked Brad.

'The old movie theatre,' he replied. 'I remember when it opened. We were all real excited. We were going to have a movie theatre! We were going to have something to do! They showed one movie and that was it. They shut it down.'

'What was the movie?' I asked.

'*Night of the Living Dead*,' said Brad.

There was a silence.

'Appropriate,' I said.

Brad scanned the remnants of Main Street. 'Al Dunlap doesn't understand how many people he hurt when he closed down the plant,' he said. 'To a small town like this? It hurt.' His face flushed with anger. 'I mean, *look* at this place,' he said.

The old Sunbeam plant was a mile out of town. It was big – the size of five football fields. In one room three hundred people used to make the toasters. In another room three hundred other people packaged them. I assumed the place would be abandoned now, but in fact a new business had moved in. They didn't have six hundred employees. They had five: five people huddled together in a vast expanse of nothingness, manufacturing lampshades.

Their boss was Stewart. He had worked at the plant

until Al Dunlap became Sunbeam's CEO and shut the place down.

'It's good to see productivity still happening in this room,' I said.

'Mm,' said Stewart, looking slightly concerned that maybe productivity wouldn't carry on happening in here for long.

Stewart and his friend Bill and Brad's friend Libby gave me the tour of the plant's emptiness. They wanted to show an outsider what happens when 'madmen take the helm of a once great company'.

'Are you talking about Al Dunlap?' I asked.

'At Sunbeam there was madman after madman,' said Stewart. (This being a book about *actual* madness I think it's probably a good idea for me to point out that Stewart and Bill are laypeople, and are using the term 'madman' in a casual way.) 'It wasn't just Dunlap. Who was the first madman? Buckley?'

'Yeah, Buckley,' said Bill.

'Buckley had a little security guy with a machine gun following him around,' said Stewart. 'He had a fleet of jets and Rolls-Royces and $10,000 ice sculptures. They were spending money freely and the company wasn't making much money.'

(I later read that Robert J. Buckley was fired as Sunbeam's CEO in 1986 after shareholders had complained that even though the company was flailing, he kept a fleet of five jets for him and his family, installed his son in a $1 million apartment at company expense and put $100,000 on the company tab for wines.)

'Who came after Buckley?' I asked.

'Paul Kazarian,' says Bill. 'I believe he was a brilliant man. Smart. A hard worker. But . . .' Bill fell silent. 'I have a story I could tell you about him, but it isn't for mixed company.'

We all looked at Libby.

'Oh, sure,' she said.

She took a long walk away from us across the barren factory floor, past cobwebs and broken window panes and skips that were empty except for dust. When she was far out of earshot Bill said, 'One time I was failing to get some sale and he screamed at me, "You should suck this bastard's DICK to get the sale!" Right in front of a room full of people. Why would he act that way? He was a foul-mouthed . . .'

Bill's face was red. He was shaking at the memory.

According to the John Byrne book *Chainsaw*, which details the history of the Sunbeam Corporation, Paul Kazarian during his tenure as CEO threw pints of orange juice over the company's controller and fired a BB gun at executives' empty chairs during board meetings. But he was also known to care about job security and workers' rights. He wanted the company to succeed without having to close down plants. He brought production jobs back from Asia and started an employees' university.

We indicated to Libby that it was OK for her to return. She did.

'And after Paul Kazarian?' I asked.

'*Then* it was Al Dunlap,' said Stewart.

'I'm seeing him tomorrow,' I said. 'I'm driving down to Ocala, Florida, to meet him.'

'What?' Stewart said, startled, his face darkening. 'He's not in jail?'

'He's in the *opposite* of jail,' I said. 'He's in a vast mansion.'

For a second I saw the veins in Stewart's neck rise up.

We headed back to Stewart's office.

'Oh,' I said. 'I was recently with a psychologist called Bob Hare. He said you could tell a lot about a business leader if you ask him a particular question.'

'OK,' he said.

'If you saw a crime-scene photograph,' I asked, 'something really horrifying, like a close-up picture of a blown-apart face, what would your response be?'

'I would back away,' Stewart replied. 'It would scare me. I would not like it. I would feel sorry for that person and I would fear for myself.' He paused. 'So what does that say about me?'

I glanced out of Stewart's window at the plant floor beyond. It was a strange sight – a tiny huddle of five lampshade manufacturers inside this great, bleak expanse. I had told Stewart how gratifying it was to see a business flourishing in here but the truth was obvious: things weren't great.

'So what does that say about me?' Stewart said again.

'Good things!' I reassured him.

Sunbeam was, in the mid-1990s, a mess. Profligate CEOs like Robert Buckley had left the company flailing. The board of directors needed a merciless cost-cutter and so they offered the job to someone unique – a man who seemed to actually, unlike most humans, *enjoy* firing people. His name was Al Dunlap and he'd made his reputation closing down plants on behalf of Scott, America's oldest toilet-paper manufacturers. There were countless stories of him going from Scott plant to Scott plant firing people in amusing, sometimes eerie ways. At a plant in Mobile, Alabama, for instance, he asked a man how long he'd worked there.

'Thirty years!' the man proudly replied.

'Why would you want to stay with a company for thirty years?' Dunlap said, looking genuinely perplexed. A few weeks later he closed the Mobile plant, firing everyone.

Dunlap's autobiography, *Mean Business*, was replete with anecdotes about firing people such as this one:

> The corporate morale officer at Scott [was] a pleasant enough person being paid an obscene amount of money, her primary job was to ensure harmony in the executive suite. The hell with harmony. These people should have been tearing each other's hair out. I told [Scott's CFO Basil] Anderson to get rid of her . . . Later that week one of the in-house lawyers fell asleep during an executive meeting. That was his last doze on our payroll. A few days later he was a memory.

And so on. He fired people with such apparent glee that the business magazine *Fast Company* included him in an article about potentially psychopathic CEOs. All the other CEOs cited were dead or in prison, and therefore unlikely to sue, but they took the plunge with Dunlap anyway, referring to his poor behavioural controls (his first wife charged in her divorce papers that he once threatened her with a knife and muttered that he always wondered what human flesh tasted like) and his lack of empathy (even though he was always telling journalists about his wise and supportive parents, he didn't turn up to either of their funerals).

On the July 1996 day that Sunbeam's board of directors revealed the name of their new CEO the share price sky-rocketed from $12.50 to $18.63. It was – according to Dunlap's unofficial biographer John Byrne – the largest jump in New York Stock Exchange history. On the day a few months later that Dunlap announced that half of Sunbeam's twelve thousand employees would be fired (according to the *New York Times* this was in percentage terms the largest work-force reduction of its kind ever) the share price shot up again, to $28. In fact the only time the price wavered during those heady months was on 2 December 1996, when *Business Week* revealed that Dunlap had failed to show up to his parents' funerals and had – according to his first wife – threatened her with a knife. On that day, the share price went down 1.5%.

It reminded me of that scene in the movie *Badlands* when fifteen-year-old Holly, played by Sissy Spacek, suddenly realizes with a jolt that her tough, handsome boy-friend Kit has actually crossed the line from rugged to lunatic. She takes an anxious step backwards but then says in her vacant monotone of a voice-over, 'I could have snuck out the back or hid in the boiler room, I suppose, but I sensed that my destiny now lay with Kit for better or for worse.'

Much as in *Badlands*, Al Dunlap's relationship with his shareholders bounced back fast after 2 December, and together they went on a year-long rampage across rural America, closing plants in Shubuta and Bay Springs and Laurel, Mississippi, and Cookeville, Tennessee, and Paragould, Arkansas, and Coushatta, Louisiana, and on and on, turning communities across the American south into ghost towns. With each plant closure the Sunbeam share price soared, reaching an incredible $51 by the spring of 1998.

Coincidentally, Bob Hare writes about *Badlands* in his seminal book on psychopathy, *Without Conscience*:

> If Kit is the moviemaker's conception of a psychopath, Holly is the real thing, a talking mask simply going through the motions of feeling deeply. Her narration is delivered in a monotone and embellished with phrases drawn straight from the glossies telling young girls what they should feel. If there was ever an example of 'knowing the words but not the music' Spacek's character is it.

It all ended for Dunlap in the spring of 1998, when the US Securities and Exchange Committee began investigating allegations that he had engineered a massive accounting fraud at Sunbeam. $60 million of the record $189 million earnings for 1997 were, they said, the result of fraudulent accounting. Dunlap denied the charges.

He demanded from Sunbeam, and was given, a massive severance pay to add to the $100 million he earned in his twenty months at Scott.

Back then, in the pre-Enron days, there wasn't quite the appetite for pursuing criminal charges when the cases were as complicated at that one was, and in 2002 Dunlap's legal troubles ended when he agreed to pay $18.5 million to settle various lawsuits. Part of his deal with the SEC was that he would never again serve as an officer or a director of a public company.

'What about his childhood?' I asked his biographer John Byrne before I set off for Shubuta. 'Are there unusual stories about odd behaviour? Getting into trouble with the police? Or torturing animals?'

'I went back to his high school but I don't believe I interviewed any of his old classmates,' he replied. 'I have no recall.'

'Oh,' I said.

'I know he was a keen boxer as a child,' he said.

'Oh?' I said.

'Yes, he made some comments about how much he enjoyed beating people up.'

'Oh REALLY?' I said.

'And his sister once said he threw darts at her dolls.'

'Oh *REALLY*?' I said.

I wrote in my notepad: '*Throws darts at sister's dolls, enjoys beating people up.*'

'What was he like when you met him?' I asked.

'I never did,' he said. 'He wouldn't see me.'

There was a short silence.

'*I'm* going to meet him,' I said.

'Are you?' he said, startled and, I think, a little jealous.

'Yes,' I said. 'Yes I *am*.'

The first obviously strange thing about Al Dunlap's grand Florida mansion and lavish, manicured lawns – he lives a ten-hour drive from Shubuta – was the unusually large number of ferocious sculptures there were of predatory animals. They were everywhere: stone lions and panthers and eagles soaring downwards, their teeth bared, and hawks with fish in their talons, and on and on, across the grounds, around the lake, in the swimming-pool/health-club complex, in the many rooms. There were crystal lions and onyx lions and iron lions and iron panthers and paintings of lions and sculptures of human skulls.

Like Toto Constant's army of plastic Burger King figurines but huge and vicious and expensive, I wrote in my reporter's notepad.

'Lions,' said Al Dunlap, showing me around. He was wearing a casual jacket and slacks and looked tanned, healthy. His teeth were very white. 'Lions. Jaguars. Lions. Always predators. Predators. Predators. Predators. I have a great belief in and a great respect for predators. Everything I did I had to go make happen.'

Item 5: Cunning/manipulative I wrote in my reporter's notepad. '*His statements may reveal a belief that the world is made up of "predators and prey", or that it would be foolish not to exploit weaknesses in others.*'

'Gold too,' I said. 'There's a lot of gold here too.'

I had been prepared for the gold, having recently

seen a portrait of him sitting on a gold chair, wearing a gold tie, with a gold suit of armour by the door and a gold crucifix on the mantelpiece.

'Well,' said Al. 'Gold is shiny. Sharks.'

He pointed at a sculpture of four sharks encircling the planet. 'I believe in predators,' he said. 'Their spirit will enable you to succeed. Over there you've got falcons. Alligators. Alligators. More alligators. Tigers.'

'It's as if both Midas and also the Queen of Narnia were here,' I said, 'and the Queen of Narnia flew above a particularly fierce zoo and turned everything there to stone and then transported everything here.'

'What?' said Al.

'Nothing,' I said.

'No,' he said, 'what did you just say?'

He shot me a steely, blue-eyed stare, which I found quite debilitating.

'It was just a jumble of words,' I said. 'I was trying to make a funny comment but it all became confused in my mouth.'

'Oh,' said Al. 'I'll show you outside. Would you like to walk or take the golf cart?'

'I think walk,' I said.

We wandered past several extravagant oil paintings of his German shepherd dogs. There was a famous seven-week period during the mid-1990s, when he was laying off the 11,200 Scott employees, that he demanded they pay for two suites at the Four Seasons Hotel in Philadelphia – one for himself and his wife, Judy, and another for his two German shepherds. He has a son,

Troy, from his first marriage but I noticed there were no pictures of him anywhere, just lots of portraits of the German shepherd dogs and grand gold-framed life-sized oil paintings of Al and Judy, both looking serious but magnanimous.

We took a walk across his lawns. I spotted Judy, standing near a stone sculpture of a sweet, tousle-haired child that overlooked the lake. She was blonde, like Al, and wearing a peach sweatsuit. She was just looking out across the lake, hardly moving.

'You visited a plant one time,' I said to Al. 'You asked a man how long he'd been working there. He said, "Thirty years." You said, "Why would you want to work at a company for thirty years?" He saw it as a badge of honour but you saw it as a negative.'

'A negative to me,' he replied. 'And here's why. If you're just going to stay someplace you become a care-taker, a custodian. Life should be a rollercoaster, not a merry-go-round.'

I wrote in my notepad, *Lack of empathy*. Then I turned to a clean page.

'Shall we get some ice tea?' he said.

On our way to the kitchen I noticed a framed poem on his desk, written in fancy calligraphy, a few lines of which read,

It wasn't easy to do
What he had to do
But if you want to be liked
Get a dog or two.

'Sean had it done for my birthday,' he said.

Sean was Sean Thornton, Al's long-term bodyguard. 'If you want to get a friend get a dog,' said Al. 'We've always had two. I hedge my bets!'

I laughed but I knew this wasn't the first time he'd used this line. It was on page xii of the preface of his autobiography, *Mean Business*: 'If you want a friend, get a dog. I'm not taking any chances; I've got two dogs.'

And in the unofficial biography, *Chainsaw*, John Byrne writes about an occasion back in 1997 that Al invited a hostile financial analyst, Andrew Shore, to his home.

> 'I so love dogs,' Dunlap said, handing Shore photographs [of his German shepherds]. 'You know, if you want a friend, you get a dog. I have two, to hedge my bets.'
>
> Shore had heard the exact line before, in one of the many articles he had read about Dunlap. But he laughed.

I wrote in my notepad, *Glibness/superficial charm*. *'He is always ready with a quick and clever comeback [but] may actually provide very little useful information.'*

(Michael Douglas says something like it in the 1987 movie *Wall Street*. He says: 'If you need a friend, get a dog. It's trench warfare out there.' I wondered if the screenwriters had taken the line from Al Dunlap, but later I discovered that he hadn't been the only bigwig to say it.

'You want a friend in Washington? Get a dog,' Harry S. Truman had apparently said during his presidency, according to the 1975 biographical play, *Give 'em Hell, Harry!*.

'You learn in this business, if you want a friend, get a dog,' said the corporate raider and pharmaceutical chief Carl Icahn at some point during the mid-1980s.

'If you want to be liked, get a dog,' said the host of CBS's *Inside Edition*, Deborah Norville, in the early 1990s. 'The people you work with are not your friends.')

We gathered in the kitchen – Al, Judy and Sean the body-guard.

I cleared my throat.

'You know how I said in my email that your amygdala might not shoot the requisite signals of fear to your central nervous system and that's perhaps why you've been so successful and so interested in the predatory spirit?'

'Yes,' he said. 'It's a fascinating theory. It's like *Star Trek*. You're going where no man has gone before. Why are some people enormously successful and others not at all? The kids I went to school with had a lot more privileges than me but they're not successful. Why? What's different? Something's different! It's a question that's been on people's minds for generations! And that's why, when you mentioned this amygdala thing, I thought, "Hmm. That's very interesting. I'll talk to this fellow." '

'I have to tell you that some psychologists say that if this part of your brain doesn't work properly it can actually make you . . .'

'Mmm?' he said.

'Dangerous,' I mumbled inaudibly.

I suddenly felt incredibly nervous. It was true that I had already asked two people – Tony and Toto – if they were psychopaths, and so I ought to have been used to doing so. But this was different. I was inside a man's mansion, not a maximum-security prison or a mental hospital.

'Sorry?' he said. 'I can't hear you.'

'Dangerous,' I said.

There was a short silence.

'In what respect?' he said, thinly.

'It can make you . . .' I took a breath. 'A psychopath.'

Al, Judy and Sean the bodyguard stared at me. For a long time. I was in over my head. What did I think I was doing? I'm not a licensed medical professional or a scientist. Nor, if I'm being honest with myself, am I actually a detective. I blamed Bob Hare. He hadn't *told* me to do this, but I never would have had I not met him. His checklist gave me false confidence that I could make my way in this land of psychopaths. I should have listened to Adam Perkins' warnings. I'm not a detective, not a psychologist, and I didn't even score that well when I self-diagnosed with the DSM-IV.

They looked at once deeply angry, befuddled and disappointed. Al had let me into his home and I was being compelled by circumstance to ask him if he was a psychopath. It is not illegal to be a psychopath but, still, it's probably very insulting to be asked if you are one.

'I've got a list of personality traits written down here that define psychopathy,' I said, pointing at my pocket.

'Who the hell are the people who make the list?' said Al. 'What are their *names*? I bet I never *heard* of them!'

At this I realized I could turn the situation around to make Bob take the blame *in absentia* for the unpleasantness.

'Bob Hare,' I said. I pronounced his name quite clearly: 'Bob Hare.'

'I never *heard* of him!' said Al, a triumphant glint in his eye.

'Never heard of him!' Judy agreed.

'He's a *psychologist*,' I said. I exhaled to indicate that I felt the same way he presumably did about psychologists.

Al pointed towards a gold cabinet in his office, inside which were photographs of him with Henry Kissinger, Donald Trump, Prince Charles, Ronald Reagan, Kerry Packer, Lord Rothschild, Rush Limbaugh and Jeb Bush as if to say, '*Those* are men I have heard of!'

'So, that list . . . ?' said Al. He looked suddenly intrigued. 'Go ahead,' he said. 'Let's do it.'

'OK,' I said. I pulled it out of my pocket. 'Are you sure?'

'Yeah, let's do it . . . '

'OK. Item 1. Superficial charm.'

'I'm totally charming,' he replied. 'I am *totally* charming!'

He, Judy and Sean laughed, easing the tension.

'Grandiose sense of self-worth?' I asked.

This would have been a hard one for him to deny, standing as he was below a giant oil painting of himself.

'*Item 2: Grandiose Sense of Self Worth*,' I had written in my notepad earlier. '*His inflated ego and exaggerated regard for his own abilities are remarkable, given the facts of his life.'*

In fact on my way here I had made a detour to Florida State University in Tallahassee, to see the Dunlap Student Success Center. It had been built with a $10 million donation from Al and was without doubt an ostentatious monument to them and their German shepherds. There was a huge painting of them and the dogs on the lobby wall in which Judy was wearing a leopard-print blouse and Al was wearing a gold tie. There was a bronze plaque into which Al's and Judy's faces had been carved above a button which, when pressed, played a recording of Al sermonizing on the subject of Leadership. (There were no good leaders left, his oration basically said, and if America wanted to survive they ought to develop some dynamic ones fast.)

I had asked Kelly, one of the building's managers, to show me around the Center.

'We are thrilled that the Dunlaps chose to give their money to an opportunity to develop citizenship and leadership and the career life story of Florida State students,' she told me.

'Al isn't known for being the most charitable person,' I replied. 'Have you reflected on why the change?'

'I can speak only to the opportunity to do good in this physical space that his gift has made possible,' she said.

'I've heard he collects sculptures of predatory animals,' I said. 'Eagles and alligators and sharks and bears. Any animal that goes, "ARGH!" It strikes me as a strange hobby. Has he ever spoken to you about that hobby?'

'We have not had an opportunity to speak to that,' she said, looking like she wanted to kill me. 'We have talked about the opportunity to be together in this space and for Florida State students to learn.'

'Al says life is all about winning,' I said. 'What do you think about that?'

'I think I am thrilled that he chose to give his charity to Florida State University and this building is a place where we can do amazing work because he's chosen to give us this opportunity and we are so thankful for that,' she said.

'Thank you very much,' I said.

'Thank *you*!' she said, wandering away.

'Grandiose sense of self-worth?' I said to Al now in his kitchen.

'No question,' said Al. 'If you don't believe in your-self, nobody else will. You've got to believe in you.'

'Is there another list of *good* things?' said Judy, quite sharply.

'Well . . .' I said. We all fell silent. 'Need for stimula-tion/proneness to boredom?' I said.

'Yeah,' said Al. 'I'm very prone to boredom. I gotta go do something. Yeah. That's a fair statement. I'm not the most relaxed person in the world. My mind does not stop working all night.'

'Manipulative?' I said.

'I think you could describe that as *leadership*,' he said. 'Inspire! I think it's called *leadership*.'

'Are you OK with this list?' I asked.

'Yeah, sure, why not?' he said.

• • •

And so the morning continued, with Al redefining a great many psychopathic traits as Leadership Positive. Impulsivity was 'just another way of saying Quick Analysis. Some people spend a week weighing up the pros and cons. Me? I look at it for ten minutes. And if the pros outweigh the cons? Go!' Shallow affect stops you from feeling 'some nonsense emotions'. A lack of remorse frees you up to move forward and achieve more great things. What's the point in drowning yourself in sorrow?

'You have to judge yourself at the end of the day,' he said. 'Do I respect me? And if you do? Fine! You've had a great run.'

'You do feel good about yourself?' I asked.

'I do!' he replied. 'Oh, I do! Looking back at my life is like going to a movie about a person who did all this *stuff*. My gosh! I did *that*? And through it all I did it my way.'

'What about the way you treated your first wife?' I asked.

'I . . .' Al furrowed his brow. He looked at me. 'I'd been at West Point,' he said. 'You go from this glamorous lifestyle to being some – ' he screwed up his face – 'young married lieutenant at some remote base some place. At that young age it's an extremely difficult transition . . .' He trailed off.

'So you saw your wife as something that was holding you back?' I said.

Al shrugged and glanced at the floor for a moment. 'I was stationed on a nuclear missile site,' he said. 'You're dealing with *nuclear weapons*. I was there during the Cuban missile crisis. The job's very serious. You've got a mission. If you fail the mission a lot of people could be seriously hurt. And does that commitment conflict with your family life? Of course it does . . .'

Al was referring to the time during the Cuban missile crisis that he left his five-month-pregnant wife home alone with no food or access to money and in desperation she had to call her mother and sister for help.

'Oh!' I said. 'One more thing. When you see a crimescene photograph – something really grotesque, someone's face blown apart or something – do you react with horror?'

He shook his head. 'No,' he said. 'I think I intellectualize it.'

'Really?' I said. 'It makes you curious? It's absorbing? Like a puzzle to be solved?'

'Curious,' nodded Al. 'As opposed to, "Oh my gosh that's frightened me!" I'm not going to go sit in the corner of the room. What enters my mind is, "What happened here? Why did it happen?" '

'Your body doesn't feel debilitated in response to the shock of seeing the picture?' I said.

Al shook his head.

I was leaning forward, peering at him over my glasses, carefully scrutinizing him. He quickly clarified, 'Yeah, what enters my mind is, what happened here and how can it be prevented from ever happening again.'

'How can it be prevented from ever happening again?' I asked.

'You cannot be a leader and cringe from evil and badness,' he said. 'You've got to *face* it.' He paused. 'The basic definition of leadership is the person who rises above the crowd and gets something done. OK?'

• • •

We had lunch before I left. Al seemed in surprisingly high spirits for a man who'd just been questioned on which psychopathic traits most applied to him. He had a little gold axe on his lapel. As we ate he told me funny stories about firing people. Each was essentially the same: someone was lazy and he fired them with an amusing quip. For instance, one lazy Sunbeam executive mentioned to him that he'd just bought himself a fabulous sports car.

'You may have a fancy sports car,' Al replied, 'but I'll tell you what you don't have. A *job*!'

Judy laughed at each of the anecdotes, though she had surely heard them many times, and I realized what a godsend to a corporation a man who enjoys firing people must be.

They took me into their TV room and showed me a speech Al once gave Florida State University on the subject of leadership. At the end of the tape Judy applauded the TV. She clearly adored her husband, adored his no-nonsense approach to life, his practically Darwinian street-smarts. I wondered what sort of woman loved a man like that.

I said, 'Tell me about the Sunbeam years— '

He cut me off.

'Sunbeam didn't work,' he shrugged. 'Sunbeam's a footnote in my career. It wasn't the biggest corporation. It had products that were a bit fickle. Appliances. I don't get too disturbed about it. In the scheme of things it's inconsequential.'

And that's all he would say about Sunbeam. We talked about Lack of Empathy. Al said he did empathize 'with people who want to make something of themselves', but unfortunately that didn't include his son Troy, or his sister, Denise.

For Denise, the relationship ended for good in January, 1994, when she called her brother to let him know that her daughter, Carolyn, a college junior, was diagnosed with leukaemia.

"Can I just know that you'll be there if I need you?" she asked him.

"No," Dunlap tersely replied, she recalls.

– John A. Byrne, *Business Week*, December 2nd 1996

'I haven't spoken to my sister in years,' he said. 'In high school I was very close to the top of the class. I was an athlete. And then I went off to West Point. And she *resented* it! To me that makes no sense. If I had a brother or an older sister I'd be so proud. I'd be, "Wow! I want to be like my brother!" Her attitude was just the opposite. "*Look what he's got*." I earned it!'

Al's relationship with Troy was just as frosty.

'I tried to help him on numerous occasions,' he shrugged. 'I tried. Honestly, I tried. It just didn't work out. And then he made some statements to the press . . .'

Upon hearing the news of his father's sacking [from Sunbeam] Troy Dunlap chortled.

"I laughed like hell," he says. "I'm glad he fell on his ass."

Dunlap's sister, Denise, his only sibling, heard the news from a friend in New Jersey. Her only thought: "He got exactly what he deserved."

– *Business Week*, 1998.

I wrote in my notepad, and then turned to a clean page so they wouldn't spot my thoughts, *Feeling no*

*remorse must be a blessing when all you have left are
your memories.*

'It's the tall-poppy thing,' Al Dunlap was calling from
across the room. 'Everyone wants to cut the tall poppy.
I'm sure since you've achieved a level of success people
are saying nasty things about you. And you're thinking,
"Wait a minute. Nobody ever gave a damn before I got
to this level." Is that true?'

'Yes. It's true,' I said.

'Screw them,' Al said. 'They're just jealous. You do
what you have to do. So, you understand?'

I glanced up at the oil painting.

Write something about Narcissus, I added on a fresh
page. *Write something about the moral barrenness of
padding around a mansion that's much too big for just
two people, a mansion filled with giant reflections of
yourself.*

I smiled to myself at the cleverness of my phraseology.

'*You* understand, right?' said Dunlap. 'You've had
some success. You're like me. When you reach a certain
level, jealous people go for you. Right? They lie about
you. They try and cut you down. You did what you had
to do to get where you've gone. We're the same.'

Also write something about the Queen of Narnia, I
wrote.

And so it was that shareholders and boards of directors
within the toaster-manufacturing world of the 1990s
came to appreciate the short-term business benefits of
employing a CEO who displayed many character traits

that would, as it transpired, score him high on the Bob Hare Psychopath Checklist.

Bob Hare was spending the night at the Heathrow Airport Hilton. He emailed me to ask how things had gone with Al Dunlap. I replied that I'd tell him in person.

I met him in the hotel bar. He was more in demand than ever, he said, now that a big study he'd co-authored, 'Corporate Psychopathy', had just been published. In it two hundred and three 'corporate professionals' were assessed with his checklist – 'including CEOs, directors, supervisors', Bob said – and the results showed that whilst the majority weren't at all psychopathic, '3.9% had a score of at least thirty, which is extremely high, even for a prison population, at least four or five times the prevalence in the general population.'

Bob clarified that we don't have a lot of empirical data for how many psychopaths are walking around in the general population, but the assumption is that it's a little less than one per cent. And so, his study showed, it is four or five times more likely that some corporate bigwig is a very high-scoring psychopath than someone just trying to earn an OK living for their family.

Over a glass of red wine I briefed him on my Al Dunlap visit. I told him how Al had pretty much confessed to a great many of the psychopathic traits, seeing them as business positives, and Bob nodded, unsurprised.

'Psychopaths say there are predators and prey,' Bob said. 'When they say that, take it as factual.'

'It's funny you should mention predators,' I said. 'Try and guess what his house was filled with.'

'Eagles,' said Bob. 'Bears . . .'

'Yes!' I said. 'Panthers. Tigers. A whole menagerie. Not stuffed. Statues. How would you *know* that?'

'I have a few insights here,' he said, pointing at his skull. 'I'm a researcher but I have clinical insights.'

Then I frowned. 'But he did tell me he cried when his dog died,' I said.

'Yeah?' said Bob.

'Yes,' I said. 'We had just had a conversation about shallow affect. He said he didn't allow himself to be weighed down by nonsense emotions. But then I was admiring an oil painting of his dog Brit and he said he cried his eyes out when it died. He said he cried and cried and cried and that meant he couldn't be a psychopath.'

I realized I was admitting this to Bob in an almost apologetic manner, as if it was sort of my fault, like I was a casting agent who had put forward an imperfect actor for a job.

'Oh, that's quite common,' said Bob.

'Really?' I said, brightening.

'Dogs are a possession,' Bob explained. 'Dogs – if you have the right dog – are extremely loyal. They're like a slave, right? They do everything you want them to. So, yeah, he cried his eyes out when his dog died. Would he cry his eyes out if his *cat* died?'

I narrowed my eyes. 'I don't think he has a cat,' I said, nodding slowly.

'He'd probably cry his eyes out if he got a dent in his car,' said Bob. 'If he had a Ferrari or a Porsche – and he probably does – and someone scratched it and kicked it he'd probably go out of his *mind* and want to kill the guy. So, yeah, the psychopath might cry when his dog dies and you think that's misplaced because he doesn't cry when his *daughter* dies.'

I was about to say, 'Al Dunlap doesn't have a daughter,' but Bob was continuing. 'When my daughter was dying it was killing me inside. She was dying of MS. I put myself inside her skin so many times and tried to experience what she was going through. And many times I said to my wife, "Boy, what an advantage to be a psychopath." A psychopath would look at his daughter and say, "This is really bad luck," and then go out and gamble and . . .'

Bob trailed off. We ordered coffee. 'With corporate psychopathy it's a mistake to look at them as neurologically impaired,' he said. 'It's a lot easier to look at them from a Darwinian slant. It all makes sense from the evolutionary perspective. The strategy is to pass on the gene pool for the next generation. Now, they don't consciously think that. They don't think, "I'm going to go out and impregnate as many women as I can," but that's the genetic imperative. So what do they do? They've got to attract women. They like women a lot. So they've got to misrepresent their resources. They've got to manipulate and con and deceive and be ready to move on as soon as things get hot.'

'Ah,' I said, frowning again. 'With Al Dunlap that really doesn't hold up. He's been married for forty-one years. There's no evidence of affairs. None at all. He's been a loyal husband. And a lot of journalists have dug around—'

'It doesn't matter,' interrupted Bob. 'We're talking in

generalities. There are lots of exceptions. What happens outside the marriage? Do you know? Do you have any idea?'

'Um,' I said.

'Does his wife have any idea what goes on outside the marriage?' Bob said. 'A lot of these serial killers are married to the same person for thirty years. They have no idea what goes on outside the marriage.'

In the clean, minimalist New York City office of an enormously wealthy moneyman – a man who would only talk to me if I promised to preserve his anonymity – I sat on my hands like a schoolboy and watched as he scrolled through my website, reading out descriptions of my various previous interviewees. There were the Special Forces soldiers in my book *The Men Who Stare At Goats* who believe they can walk through walls and kill goats just by staring at them. There were the conspiracy theorists in my book *Them: Adventures With Extremists* who believe that the secret rulers of the world are giant paedophile blood-drinking reptiles from another dimension who have adopted human form.

'Wow,' he said, shaking his head in disbelief. 'I feel out of place even speaking with you. Wow. I'm about as boring a person as you're ever going to chat with.'

He indicated his office, which was indeed filled with nothing crazy. In fact it was filled with nothing at all. The desks and chairs were contoured in such a way to suggest they were impossibly expensive.

This man, who I will call Jack, witnessed the Al Dunlap affair close up. He was around when a co-owner of the company, the billionaire financier and philanthropist Michael Price – at $1.4 billion the five hundred and sixty-second richest person in the world – lobbied to get Dunlap appointed as CEO, and, Al's reputation preceding him, everyone knew what that would mean.

'I disagreed with the job cuts,' said Jack. 'I said, "Don't blame the people and the number of people." You ever seen what happens to a community when you close a facility?'

'I went to Shubuta,' I said.

'I've been to these places,' said Jack. 'I've stayed at little inns. I've been to the schools. I've been to the training centres and the tech areas. It's a joy. It really is a joy to go to these places. And then to see Wall Street applaud as they got destroyed . . .' Jack tailed off. 'If you look at any research report from the time it's so transparent to anyone who understands what's going on . . .'

'What do you mean by "research report"?' I asked.

The 'research reports' – Jack explained – are written by hedge funds and pension funds and investment banks, advising their clients on which companies to invest in.

'Wall Street, or the darker side that writes these research reports, *lionized* the job cuts in places like Shubuta,' said Jack. 'If you look at the community of support – if you were to grab research reports of the time – you'd be amazed at the comments.'

'Like what?'

'The level of callous jubilance over what he was doing. You'd probably wonder whether society had gone mad.'

'I guess those research reports are lost to the sands of time now,' I said.

'It might be possible to grab some of them,' he said. 'It was like in the Colosseum. You had the entire crowd egging him on. So who really is the villain? Is it the one who's making the cuts? Is it the analysts who are touting it? Is it the pension funds and the mutual funds who are buying?'

'Of course that was all twelve years ago now,' I said. 'Has anything changed?'

'Not anything,' Jack said. 'Zero. And it's not just in the US. It's everywhere. It's all over the world.'

A few weeks passed and then, as he promised, Jack dug up and sent me one of the research reports. He said he hoped I would agree it made for extraordinarily cold-blooded and bullish reading. It was from Goldman Sachs, dated September 19th 1996. It read:

> We reaffirm our trading buy rating on SOC (Sunbeam) shares based on the company's pending turnaround/restructuring, with CEO Al Dunlap leading the charge.

Jack had double underlined the next part to indicate just how shocking it was:

> Our EPS ests do not reflect SOC's pending restructuring and are <u>unchanged</u> at 25c for 1996 and 90c for 1997.

And then, finally, underlined and circled with an exclamation mark:

P/E on Nxt FY: 27.5X

'P/E on Nxt FY: 27.5X' was the cruellest line in the paper, Jack had said. I found it incomprehensible. When I see phrases like that my brain collapses in on itself. But this being the secret formula to the brutality, the equation that led to the death of Shubuta, I asked some financial experts to translate it.

'So,' emailed Paul J. Zak, of the Center for Neuroeconomic Studies in Claremont, California, 'the PE is the average price of the stock divided by next year's forecasted earnings. The increase in the PE means that the stock price was expected to rise faster than the increase in earnings. This means the investment house expected that the Draconian cuts would produce higher earnings for years to come, and next year's stock price would reflect that higher earnings for years in the future.'

'For a company making low-priced appliances,' emailed John A. Byrne of *Business Week*, 'it's a very high PE. The analyst is assuming that if Dunlap can squeeze out overhead and expenses, the earnings will shoot up and investors who get in early will make a killing.'

'Bottom line,' emailed Paul J. Zak. 'One investment house thought that most investors would cheer mass layoffs at Sunbeam. This is a remorseless view of people losing jobs. The only upside of this is that whomever followed this advice was seriously pissed at the investment house a year later when the stock tanked.'

As I glanced at the phraseology of the research report, dull and unfathomable to outsiders like me, I thought, 'If you have the ambition to become a villain, the first thing you should do is learn to be impenetrable. Don't act like Blofeld – monocled and ostentatious. We journalists love writing about eccentrics. We hate writing about impenetrable, boring people. It makes us look bad: the duller the interviewee, the duller the prose. If you want to get away with wielding true, malevolent power, be boring.'

7

THE RIGHT SORT
OF MADNESS

It was a week after I returned from Florida. I was sitting in a bar in North London with a friend – the documentary maker Adam Curtis – and I was animatedly telling him about Al Dunlap's crazy sculpture collection of predatory animals and his giant oil paintings of himself and so on.

'How's Elaine dealing with your new hobbyhorse?' he asked me.

Elaine is my wife. 'Oh, she likes it,' I said. 'Usually, as you know, she finds my various obsessions quite annoying, but not this time. In fact I've taught her how to administer the Bob Hare Checklist and she's already identified lots of people we know as psychopaths. Oh, I think A. A. Gill's baboon-killing article displays . . .' I paused and said, darkly: '. . . psychopathic characteristics.'

I named one or two of our mutual friends as people we now thought were psychopaths. Adam looked despairing.

'How long did it take you to get to Al Dunlap's house?' he asked me.

I shrugged. 'Ten hours on the plane,' I said. 'Plus a round trip by car to Shubuta, Mississippi, which took about another fifteen or sixteen hours.'

'So you travelled thousands of miles just to chronicle the crazy aspects of Al Dunlap's personality,' said Adam.

There was a short silence.

'Yes,' I said.

I peered at Adam. 'Yes I did,' I said, defiantly.

'You're like a medieval monk,' Adam said, 'stitching together a tapestry of people's craziness. You take a little bit of craziness from up there and a little bit of craziness from over there and then you stitch it all together.'

There was another short silence.

'No I don't,' I said.

Why was Adam criticizing my journalistic style, questioning my entire project?

'Adam is such a contrarian,' I thought. 'Such a polemicist. If he starts picking apart my thesis after I've been working on this big story for so long now, I'm not going to listen because he's a known contrarian. Yes. If Adam picks apart my thesis I won't listen.'

(Item 16: *Failure to accept responsibility for own actions—He usually has some excuse for his behavior, including rationalization and putting the blame on others.*)

'We all do it,' Adam was continuing. 'All journalists. We create stories out of fragments. We travel all over the world, propelled onwards by *something*, we sit in people's houses, our notepads in our hands, and we wait for the *gems*. And the gems invariably turn out to be the madness – the extreme, outermost aspects of that person's personality – the irrational anger, the anxiety, the paranoia, the narcissism, the things that would be defined within DSM as mental disorders. We've dedicated our lives to it. We know what we do is odd but nobody talks about it. Forget psychopathic CEOs. My question is, what does all this say about *our* sanity?'

I looked at Adam and I scowled. Deep down, although I was massively reluctant to admit it, I knew he was right. For the past year or more I had travelled to Gothenburg and Broadmoor and upstate New York and Florida and Mississippi, driven by my compulsion to root out craziness. I thought back on my time with Al Dunlap, about the vague disappointment I felt whenever he had said things to me that were *reasonable*. There had been a moment before our lunch, for instance, when I'd asked him about Items 12 and 18 – *Early behavior problems* and *Juvenile delinquency*.

'Lots of successful people rebelled against their teachers or parents!' I'd prompted. 'There's nothing wrong with *that*!'

But he'd replied, 'No. I was a focused, serious kid. I was very determined. I was a good kid. In school I was always trying to achieve. I was always working hard.

That saps your energy. You don't have enough time to trouble-make.'

'You never got into trouble with the authorities?' I said.

'No,' he said. 'And, remember, I got accepted into West Point. Listen. The psychopath thing is rubbish. You cannot be successful unless you have certain' – he pointed at his head – '*controls*. It won't happen. How do you get through school? How do you get through your first and second job when you're formulating yourself?'

It was a terribly persuasive point and I had felt disappointed when he said it. Also, he denied being a liar ('If I think you're a schmuck I'll tell you you're a schmuck'), and having a parasitic lifestyle ('I go get my own meal'), and even though he was against 'nonsense emotions', he did feel 'the right emotions'. Furthermore, his $10 million donation to Florida State University might have been narcissistic but it was also a nice gesture. And he really did have a loyal wife of forty-one years. There really were no rumours of affairs. This would score him a zero on Items 17 and 11, *Many short-term marital relationships* and *Promiscuous sexual behavior.*

Of course even the highest-scoring psychopath would score zero on some of the items on Bob's checklist. What jolted me was my own strange craving as a journalist and also as a now qualified psychopath-spotter to see Al Dunlap in *absolute* terms.

I mulled over what Adam had said to me: '*We all do it. We wait for the gems. And the gems invariably turn out to be the madness.*' We had both assumed that journalists do this instinctively. We have an inherent understanding of what makes a good interview moment and the last thing on our minds is whether it is a manifestation of a catalogued mental disorder.

But I suddenly wondered, what if some of us journalists go about it in the opposite way? What if some of us have grasped that sufferers of certain mental disorders make the most electrifying interviewees and have devised clever, covert, Bob Hare-like methods of identifying them?

And so in the days that followed I asked around. I asked editors and guest-bookers and TV producers.

And that's how I came to hear about a woman named Charlotte Scott.

Charlotte lives in a lovely, quite idyllic, old, low-beamed cottage in Kent. Her ten-week-old baby snored gently in the corner of the room. She was on maternity leave but even so, she said, her TV-producing days were behind her. She was out now and she'd never go back.

She was at one time, she said, an idealist. She'd wanted to get into crusading journalism but somehow ended up working as an assistant producer on a British shopping channel called bid-up.tv – 'My glittering career,' she sighed – but eventually she made a leap upwards to mainstream TV as a guest-booker for the sort of television programmes where extended families mired in drama and tragedy yell at each other in front of a studio audience. She thought her old friends who poked fun at her career path were snobs. This was journalism for the people. And anyway, important social issues were raised on the shows every day. Drugs. Incest. Adultery. Cross-dressing. That sort of thing. She began hanging out more with her fellow guest-bookers than her old university friends.

'What did your job entail?' I asked her.

'We had a hotline,' Charlotte explained. 'Families in crisis who want to be on TV called the hotline. My job was to call them back, repeatedly, over a matter of weeks, even if they'd changed their minds and decided not to do the show. There had to be a show. You had to keep going.'

Of course lots of jobs involve relentlessly calling people back. It is soul-destroying – 'Honestly, it was awful,' Charlotte said, 'I mean, I'd been to university' – but not unusual.

At first all the tragedy she had to listen to over the phone would grind her down. But you need to be hard and focused to be a good researcher so she devised ways to detach herself from her potential interviewees' misery.

'We started to laugh at these people,' she explained. 'All day long. It was the only way we could cope. Then in the evening we would go to a bar and scream with laughter some more.'

'What kind of jokes did you make about them?' I asked her.

'If they had a speech impediment, that would be brilliant,' she said. 'We put them on loudspeaker and gathered round and laughed and laughed.'

And, sure enough, Charlotte soon began to 'feel removed from the person on the other end of the phone'.

Of course lots of people dehumanize others – find

ways to eradicate empathy and remorse from their day jobs – so they can perform their jobs better. That's presumably why medical students tend to throw human cadavers at each other for a joke, and so on.

The thing that made Charlotte truly unusual was the brainwave she came up with one day. It had dawned on her early on in her career that, yes, the show's best guests were the ones that were mad in certain ways. And one day she realized that there was a brilliantly straightforward way of seeking them out. Her method was far more rudimentary than the Bob Hare Checklist, but just as effective for her requirements. It was this: 'I'd ask them what medication they were on. They'd give me a list. Then I'd go to a medical website to see what they were for. And I'd assess if they were too mad to come onto the show or just mad enough.'

'Just mad enough?' I asked.

'Just mad enough,' said Charlotte.

'What constituted *too* mad?' I asked.

'Schizophrenia,' said Charlotte. 'Schizophrenia was a no-no. So were psychotic episodes. If they're on lithium for psychosis we probably wouldn't have had them on. We wouldn't want them to come on and then go off and *kill* themselves.' Charlotte paused. 'Although if the story was *awesome* – and by awesome I mean a far-reaching mega family argument that's going to make a really charged show – they would have to be pretty mad to be stopped.'

'So what constituted *just mad enough*?' I asked.

'Prozac,' said Charlotte. 'Prozac's the perfect drug. They're upset. I say, "Why are you upset?" "I'm upset because my husband's cheating on me so I went to the doctor and he gave me Prozac." Perfect! I know she's not *that* depressed, but she's depressed enough to go to a doctor and so she's probably angry and upset.'

'Did you get disappointed on the occasions you found they were on no drug at all?' I asked Charlotte. 'If they were on no drug at all did that mean they probably weren't mad enough to be entertaining?'

'Exactly,' said Charlotte. 'It was better if they were on something like Prozac. If they were on no drug at all, that probably meant they weren't mad enough.'

And that was Charlotte's secret trick. She said she didn't stop to consider *why* some sorts of madness were better than others: 'I just knew on an innate level who would make good television. We all did. *Big Brother*. *The X-Factor*. *American Idol*. *Wife Swap* . . . *Wife Swap* is particularly bad because you're monkeying with people's families, with their *children*. You've got some loop-the-

loop stranger yelling at someone's *children*. The producers spend three weeks with them, pick the bits that are
mad enough, ignore the bits that aren't mad enough, and
then leave.'

Of course reality TV is littered with the corpses of people who turned out to be the wrong sort of mad. Take
the especially sad tale of a Texan woman named Kelli
McGee. Her sister Deleese was to be a contestant on
ABC's *Extreme Makeover*. Deleese was not an attractive
woman: she had crooked teeth, a slightly deformed jaw,
and other flaws. Still, she had a tactful and considerate
family, people like her sister Kelli, who always told her
she was pretty. But she knew in her heart she wasn't and
so she applied for *Extreme Makeover*, dreaming of what
the show promised – a 'Cinderella-like' makeover to
'transform the life and destiny' of a different 'ugly duckling' each week. Deleese was, to her delight, chosen, and
the family were flown to LA for the surgical procedure
and the taping.

A section of the show always involves the ugly
duckling's family telling the camera, pre-Cinderella
transformation, just how ugly she is. The point of it is
that when she finally emerges Cinderella-like from the
makeover her journey will be more epic and emotional.
We'll see the stunned and joyful looks in the eyes of
the family members who had been embarrassed by the
ugliness but are awed by the beauty. Everyone goes home
empowered.

With Deleese's family, though, there was a problem.
They'd grown so used to diplomatically protecting her

feelings, the insults didn't come easy. They had to be coached by the programme makers. Eventually, they admitted, yes, Deleese *was* ugly: 'I never believed my son would marry such an ugly woman,' Deleese's mother-in-law agreed to say. Kelli, too, was coached to reveal how embarrassed she'd felt growing up with such an ugly sister. The boys all laughed at her and ridiculed her. And so on.

Deleese was in the next room, listening to it all on a monitor, looking increasingly shocked. Still, it would be fine: she'd get her Cinderella-like makeover. She would be beautiful.

A few hours later – just before Deleese was due to go under the surgeon's knife – a producer came in to tell her she had been axed. The production manager had done the maths and realized her recovery time wouldn't fit with the programme's budgeted schedule.

Deleese burst into tears. 'How can I go home as ugly as I left?' she cried. 'I was supposed to come home *pretty*!'

The producer shrugged, apologetically.

The family all flew back to Texas, and everything spiralled. Too many things that should have remained unsaid had now been said. Deleese sank into a depression.

'My family, who had never said anything before, said things that made me realize, "Yes, I was right and everyone did think I looked like a freak,"' she explained in her lawsuit against ABC. Finally Kelli, who suffered from bipolar disorder, felt so guilty about her part in the mess she took an overdose of pills and alcohol and died.

• • •

You might think that Charlotte, over in England, with her ostensibly foolproof secret medication-listing trick, would be immune to inadvertently booking guests who were the wrong sort of mad. But you would be mistaken.

'We once had a show called "My Boyfriend Is Too Vain",' she said. 'I pushed the vain boyfriend for the details of his vanity. Push push push. He drinks body-builder shakes all the time. He does the whole Charles Atlas. We put him on. Everyone laughs at him. Couple of days later he calls me up and while he's on the phone to me he slices open his wrists. He has severe body dys-morphic disorder, of course. I had to stay on the phone with him while we waited for the ambulance to arrive.' Charlotte shuddered. 'It was awful,' she said.

As I left Charlotte's house that afternoon and drove back to London I thought, 'Well, at least I haven't done any-thing as bad as the things Charlotte has done.'

8

THE MADNESS OF DAVID SHAYLER

One morning in July 2005 Rachel North, who works in advertising, got on the Piccadilly Line tube in Finsbury Park, North London. It was, she later told me, the most rammed carriage she had ever been on.

'More and more people were pushing on,' she said, 'and I was standing there thinking, "This is ridiculous," and then the train trundled off, and it went for about forty-five seconds, and then there was . . .' Rachel paused '. . . an explosion. I was about seven or eight feet away from it. I felt this huge power smashing me to the floor. And everything went dark. You could hear the brakes screaming and clattering. It was like being on an out-of-control fairground ride but in the dark. And it was hot. You couldn't breathe. The air was thick with smoke. And I was suddenly very wet. I was on the floor and there were people lying on top of me. And then the screaming started.'

Three years earlier, in 2002, Rachel had been violently attacked by a stranger in her home. She wrote an article about it for *Marie Clare* magazine. That's what she was doing the moment the bomb exploded: standing on a packed tube train reading the just-published *Marie Clare* article about her violent attack. As she lay on the floor she thought, 'Not again.'

They evacuated the train. Rachel was one of the last people off.

'As I climbed out into the tunnel I did a quick sweep behind me and I did see some of what had happened, and yes, that has remained with me, because I still worry whether I should have stayed, and helped, but it was so dark. I saw bent metal. There were people on the floor. There was – I won't say what I saw.'

'How many people died in your carriage?' I asked Rachel.

'Twenty-six people,' she said.

Rachel was walking wounded. She had a piece of metal embedded in her wrist deep enough for her to see the bone, but that was about it. The carriage had been so packed the people closest to the bomber had taken most of the force of the blast.

When she got home from the hospital she started blogging. She wrote and wrote, a torrent of blog postings. Of course thousands of blogs about the July 7th attacks went up that day – there were four bombs in all, three on tube trains and one on a bus, and fifty-six people died, including the four suicide bombers – but Rachel's was unique. No other blogger had been so caught up in the events, so close to the bombs, actually in the same carriage as one, plus her writings were immediate and powerful and evocative, and so her site began to attract fans.

THURSDAY JULY 7TH 2005.

. . . Everything went totally black and clouds of choking smoke filled the tube carriage and I thought I had been blinded. It was so dark nobody could see anything. I thought I was about to die, or was dead. I was choking from the smoke and felt like I was drowning . . .

SATURDAY JULY 9TH 2005.

. . . Couldn't stop watching news. When I heard that the bomb was IN MY CARRIAGE I just flipped. I was alternately pounding with anger and adrenaline and having mini-flashbacks, then feeling falling over tired. I drank several whiskies . . .

'By typing it down it was like cleaning a wound,' Rachel said. 'I was picking all the grit and the smoke out of my mind.'

Other survivors found her blog. They began leaving supportive messages for one another on it. Eventually someone pointed out that they may have been chatting away but they were doing it all alone in their respective rooms. The Internet was giving them the illusion they that were being gregarious, but in fact they were performing an empty, unsatisfying facsimile of it. They were becoming isolated and angry. Why didn't they do the old-fashioned thing and meet in real life, in the flesh? So they began to, once a month, in a pub in King's Cross.

'Some of us found we were unable to feel any joy in being alive,' Rachel said. 'Every time we went to sleep we had nightmares, of banging our hands against the glass of the train, battering away, trying to smash our way out of this train that was filled with smoke. Remember we all thought we were going to die, entombed in the smoke. And none of us had expected it.' Rachel paused for a second, then she said: 'We'd all just been on our way to work.'

After a while they decided they wanted to do more than just meet for a monthly drink. They wanted to become a pressure group. They wanted to know if the attacks could have been prevented, if Intelligence had been botched. They gave themselves a name: Kings Cross United. She carried on writing her blog.

And this was when things began to get strange. People she didn't know started posting cryptic comments she didn't understand on her site.

'You can install a thing that tells you where your visitors are coming from,' she said, 'and I noticed a few weeks after installing it that I was getting an awful lot of hits from a particular website. So I went to look at it.'

It took Rachel a while to grasp what she was reading. Somebody had taken some phrases she'd written – 'Totally black' and 'It was so dark nobody could see anything' – and was using them to suggest she wasn't describing a bomb (a bomb would have caused fire, which would have illuminated the carriage) but some kind of 'power surge'. The writer complimented Rachel on her 'courage' for whistle-blowing the true story of the power surge.

Rachel read on. These people evidently believed an accidental power surge had coursed through the London Underground that morning and that the British government wanted to cover up this corporate manslaughter by blaming it on Islamic suicide bombers. These conspiracy theorists were part of a much wider group – the 9/11 truth movement – which had become vast. Conspiracy theories were no longer just to be found, as they had pre-9/11, on the fringes of society. Now everyone knew someone who was convinced 9/11 was an inside job. They were armchair Agatha Christie sleuths, meeting on forums, sending each other YouTube links, telling each other they were right. Only the most extreme magical-thinkers amongst them were 7/7 conspiracy theorists too: whilst 9/11 obviously wasn't an inside job, 7/7 *obviously* wasn't an inside job. And now these people had brought Rachel's blog into it.

As Rachel read all of this she wondered how they'd account for the Tavistock Square bus bombing. When Hasib Hussain blew himself up on the No. 30 from Marble Arch to Hackney Wick at 9.47 a.m. the explosion ripped the roof off the top deck. The thirteen passengers who happened to have been standing at the rear of the bus died with him. There were photographs of blood and flesh on the walls of the nearby British Medical Association headquarters. How would the conspiracy theorists account for *that*?

And then Rachel saw their explanation: the bus hadn't really exploded. It was actually a fake stunt, using fancy pyrotechnics and stuntmen and actors and special-effects blood.

It's obvious what Rachel *should* have done: nothing. It shouldn't have come as a bolt from the blue that people were wrong on the Internet. But she'd just survived a terrorist attack, and maybe she was spending too much time alone in her room staring at her computer; whatever, she wasn't thinking rationally. She wasn't about to do the sensible thing.

'By that stage,' Rachel said, 'I'd met people who had lost loved ones on that bus. To call the people on the bus who died actors and stuntmen was, I thought, abhorrent. So I read all this stuff, and then I came up for air, and I thought, "They don't realize. As soon as they actually talk to a real person, someone who's been there, they'll realize it's a load of old nonsense and they'll give up." He was inviting comments on his website. So I left a very angry one: "How *dare* you misquote me in this way. Power surges do not tear people's legs off." And he responded by saying, "You didn't even know the bomb was *in your carriage*! You keep *changing your story*!" '

Rachel was furious. She felt it was her duty to make them understand they were wrong.

'But I had no idea, then, what these people were like,' she said. 'What comes through again and again is this *complete* lack of empathy. They would, for example, cut and paste the most harrowing descriptions by emergency services officers of going into carriages and seeing buckled walls that were streaming with blood and pieces of human flesh and stepping over body parts and stepping over the hole where the bomb had torn a crater in the floor. They'd post this and you couldn't read it without wanting to weep, and then they would say, "Ah! See? The hole appears to be on the *right*-hand side." And that would be their comment.'

'They were only interested in the crater?' I asked.

'Just weird,' said Rachel.

'*Item 8: Callous/lack of empathy*,' I couldn't help suspecting, although I felt differently about Bob's checklist now. I now felt that the checklist was a powerful and intoxicating weapon which was capable of inflicting terrible damage if placed in the wrong hands. I was beginning to suspect that my hands might be the wrong hands. But, still: '*Item 8: Callous/lack of empathy – Any appreciation of the pain of others is merely abstract.*'

Rachel discovered too late that by engaging with the conspiracy theorists she herself became part of the conspiracy.

'They all started discussing me,' she said. 'They formed the most bizarre theories about me. They decided that because I had this group that I'd set up, and I had this blog that I'd set up, I was feeding the official story to the survivors, and I was somehow controlling them, and I was a government mouthpiece who'd been tasked with disseminating disinformation. They became very suspicious of me. They formed this theory that I was some kind of counter-intelligence professional or security-services covert operative. Some of them thought I didn't even *exist*. They thought I was a team of men who had been tasked with creating this Rachel North persona and maintaining it as a means of what they called psy-ops – psychological operations – to control the population of the UK.'

The 'Rachel North Doesn't Exist' theory came about after some of the conspiracy theorists counted the number of posts and messages she'd left and mathematically determined that she couldn't be a single human being. She had to be a team.

Rachel tried telling them they were fantasists and that it wasn't nice to find yourself a character in another person's paranoid fantasy especially when you've just been blown up on the tube, but it was to no avail. The more prolifically she tried to convince them she existed, the more certain they became that she didn't.

'I do not work for the government,' she wrote to them. 'I am a normal person, I have a normal job in a normal office and I am requesting politely that you drop this and stop making accusations that are not true. Please stop.'

'It should be clear from Rachel's disinfo tactics she's part of the same lying media and police who set up this scam,' someone replied.

'Bet it ain't even female,' someone else agreed.

It escalated. She received death threats from them. She had almost been killed – she ran a support group for people who had almost been killed – and now they were sending her death threats. They contacted her parents, sent them information regarding the 'truth' about their daughter and July 7th. Rachel's father, who was a country vicar, found the letters upsetting and confusing.

So Rachel decided to confront them. She would show them what she looked like. In the flesh. She read they were having a meeting in the upstairs room of a pub and so she turned up with a friend. As she climbed the stairs she felt worried about what these ferocious Internet presences would be like. She imagined them to be physically menacing. And then she reached the top of the stairs and opened the door and saw a room filled with quiet, small, nerdy-looking men. Some were staring awkwardly into their pints. Others were surreptitiously glancing at them, intrigued and delighted to see that two quite glamorous-looking women had apparently joined their movement.

Rachel and her friend sat down at a table near the wall. Nothing happened for a while. And then the door opened and another man came in. He looked quite commanding, quite impressive. And Rachel recognized him immediately. She was astonished.

It was David Shayler.

David Shayler: in 1997 an MI5 spy, codenamed G9A/1, went on the run after passing secret intelligence to the *Mail on Sunday*. He had, the newspaper reported, been at an inter-agency meeting where an MI6 officer, codenamed PT16B, had announced a plan to covertly assassinate the Libyan leader, Colonel Gadaffi. The assassins were ready, PT16B had told G9A/1. They were members of an organization called the Libyan Islamic Fighting Group. They would place a bomb under a road they knew Gadaffi was scheduled to drive down. But they needed money for bomb-making equipment and food, etc., which was why they had approached MI6.

PT16B (whose name, it emerged, was David Watson) had brought G9A/1 (whose name was David Shayler) into the 'need to know group' for one simple reason: MI6 didn't want MI5 to start chasing after the assassins if they came into contact with them in some other context. The British government wasn't to know, David Watson told David Shayler. This was to be strictly covert.

Shayler thought it was probably all hot air, that David Watson was a bit of a James Bond wannabe fantasist, and nothing would come of it. But then, a few weeks later, a bomb *was* detonated under Gadaffi's cavalcade. As it transpired, the wrong car was targeted. Several bodyguards died but Gadaffi himself escaped unharmed.

Shayler was outraged. He didn't want to be part of an agency culture that involved itself in clandestine assassinations, so he decided to make a stand. He called a friend who put him onto a journalist who worked for the *Mail on Sunday*. He told him everything, received £20,000 in return, and the following Saturday night, the night before the story appeared, promptly went on the run with his girlfriend, Annie Machon.

They went first to Holland, and then on to a French farmhouse in the middle of nowhere. There was no TV, no car. They stayed there for ten months, living off the *Mail on Sunday* money. He wrote a novel. They went to Paris for a weekend, and as they stepped into the hotel lobby six men – French secret service – surrounded Shayler.

He spent four months in a French high-security jail, and then another month in a British jail before being released, a hero to the legions of people who believed he had done a valiant thing, sacrificed his liberty in a stance against illegal secret government activities. Rachel North admired him from afar. So did I.

• • •

And now, five years later, David Shayler had, to Rachel's enormous surprise, entered the upstairs room of that quite sleazy pub. What was he *doing* there, mingling with the conspiracy theorists?

And then it became clear: he was one of them.

He was the main speaker of the night. His credentials as a former MI5 officer gave him gravitas. The others listened intently. He said 7/7 never happened. It was a lie. There were vigorous nods from the crowd. The world had been fooled by a brilliant lie. Rachel couldn't take it any longer. She stood up.

'I was in the *carriage*!' she shouted.

Around that very same time, in another part of London, I happened to be looking myself up on Google when I came across a lengthy and animated discussion thread entitled 'Jon Ronson: Shill or Stupid?'. It was in response to something I'd written about how I didn't believe 9/11 was an inside job. The people on the thread were split. Some thought I was a shill (a stooge in the pay of the shadowy elite), others thought I was just stupid. I got very annoyed and left a message saying I was in fact neither a shill nor stupid. Almost immediately a few of them posted messages warning the others to beware of me because I was clearly 'another Rachel North'.

'Who's Rachel North?' I thought.

I typed her name into Google. And that's how we ended up meeting.

I spent an afternoon at her home. It was just an

ordinary house, not far from mine. She told me the whole story, from the day of the explosions through to the moment everyone started yelling at each other in the pub. It was over for her now, she said. She wasn't going to engage with them any more. She didn't want to be on the radar of crazy people. She was going to wind down her blog and stop defining herself as a victim. The last thing she said to me when I left that afternoon was, 'I know I exist.' She looked at me. 'All the people on the train who have met me know I exist. I got off the train covered in blood and smoke and glass in my hair and metal sticking out of my wrist-bone. I was photographed. I gave evidence to the police. I was stitched up in a hospital. I can produce dozens of witnesses who know I was there and that I exist. And that I am who I say I am.'

There was a short silence.

'There is no doubt that you definitely exist,' I said.

And for a second Rachel seemed to look relieved.

I emailed David Shayler. Would he like to meet with me to talk about Rachel North?

'Yes, sure,' he replied.

We got together a few days later in a cafe just off the Edgware Road, in West London. He looked tired, unhealthy, overweight, but what was most striking was how fast he talked. It was as if he couldn't contain all the words that needed to be said. They tumbled out of him, like when you get a motorbike for the first time and you accelerate too hard and you just shoot off.

He didn't talk fast at the beginning of our conversation. This was when I asked him about the old days, about how he first got his job with MI5. He smiled and relaxed and the story he told was spellbinding.

'I was looking for work and I saw an advert in the media section of the *Independent* saying *Godot Isn't Coming*,' he said. 'Having studied the play in English and French I read on. It sounded like an advert for a job in journalism, so I sent off a CV.'

His CV was good but not amazing: Dundee University, where he edited the student newspaper, a career running an eventually failed small publishing business . . . Still, he was called in for an interview with a recruitment consultancy. It was all quite ordinary.

But the second interview wasn't ordinary at all.

'It took place in an unmarked building on Tottenham Court Road, in London,' he said. 'The building was completely empty. There was nobody else there apart from one guy at reception and the one guy who interviewed me. He really was like an intelligence officer from Central Casting – pinstripe suit, tall, patrician, swept-back grey hair. You're in this crazy building with this bloke asking you all these questions.'

David had, like I had, walked down the Tottenham Court Road a million times. It is unremarkable: discount electrical shops and *Time Out* magazine. The last thing you'd expect is some parallel spook universe unfolding just behind some unmarked door.

'What questions did he ask you?' I said.

'Whether I had any religious beliefs when I was twelve. How I formed my political beliefs through my teenage years. What had been the milestones on my journey? What were the points in my life when I believed I'd done something useful? It was of a much higher level than a normal job interview. He asked me about the ethics of intelligence. He kept saying, "Why do you think you're here?" I didn't want to say it. I didn't want to look like an idiot. But he kept asking the question. Finally I said, "Is it MI5?" He said, "Of *course* it is." '

For a while after that David became paranoid. Was the whole thing some complicated charade designed to destroy him?

'I kept imagining him suddenly saying, "We spotted you a mile off and now you can fuck off!" ' David laughed. ' "We're going to ruin your life!" '

I laughed. 'That's exactly the kind of crazy thoughts I have!' I said. 'Really! I have thoughts like that! They can be quite intrusive!'

('Intrusive Thoughts' are all over DSM-IV, by the way, as symptoms of Obsessive Compulsive Disorder and Generalized Anxiety Disorder, etc., all the disorders characterized by an overactive amygdala. I used to see them as positive things: journalists *should* be quite obsessive and paranoid, shouldn't we? But ever since I read about 'Intrusive Thoughts' in DSM-IV I've found the idea a little scary, like they're something serious. I don't have them *all* the time, by the way. I wouldn't want you to think that. Just sometimes. Maybe one a week. Or less.)

MI5 offered David the job. Later he asked how many other people were recruited from that *Godot Isn't Coming* advert, and they told him none. Just him.

He was, he discovered on his first day, to be an office-based spy, in a quite mundane room, nowhere near as entrancing as his conspiracy-minded friends imagined life inside a shadowy organization like MI5 would be. (David was not a conspiracy theorist at all back then. He only became one later, when he was out of the demystifying world of shadowy elites and back in everyday life.)

'It was just a perfectly normal office,' he said. 'You've got an in-tray and an out-tray. You process information. The difference is if you don't process the information correctly, people die. I was happy to be making the world a safer place, stopping men of violence. It was good work.' But it was not without its weirdness: 'They had files on all sorts of people, like John Lennon and Ronnie Scott and most of the people who would eventually end up in the Labour cabinet. People were being accused of communism for all sorts of stupid reasons. There was a file on a twelve-year-old kid who'd written to the Communist Party saying he was doing a topic on communism at school and could they send some information? They'd got him down as a suspected communist sympathizer.'

'Would this kid ever have known MI5 had a file on him?' I asked.

'No, of course not,' David said.

From time to time he'd go out into the field, but not often. 'One time I went to a demonstration dressed as an anarchist. This guy thrust a leaflet in my hand going, "What do you know about the Anti-Election Alliance?" which I was then studying in MI5. I felt like saying to him, "A lot more than you do, mate." '

We talked about his now famous covert meeting with

PT16B, about the plot to assassinate Gadaffi, the flight to Europe, the months on the run, the arrest and imprisonment, and then the conversation turned to Rachel North. He was, he said, still convinced she didn't exist.

'Let me talk about Rachel North being a composite MI5 person,' he said. 'That's exactly the kind of thing the intelligence services would do.'

'But you've met her,' I said.

'Yes, I know I've *met* her,' he said. His voice was rising now, getting faster. 'She may exist as a human being but that's not to say there aren't five people behind her posting in her name on the Internet.'

'Oh, come *on*,' I said.

'You should look at the evidence of her copious postings,' David said. 'You should look at the evidence of how many posts she was doing at one point.'

'She was posting a lot,' I said. 'I have no doubt of that.'

'People in the movement have come to the conclusion that there were far too many posts to have come from one person,' David said.

'Oh, you know what bloggers are like,' I said. 'They write and write and write. I don't know why because they're not being paid.'

'I am also very suspicious of the fact that she refuses to sit down and have a dispassionate briefing about 7/7,' David said. 'Why won't she allow somebody to patiently talk her though the evidence?'

'She was in the *carriage*!' I said. 'She was in the *CARRIAGE*. You really want her to sit down with someone who was on the *Internet* while she was in the *carriage* and have them explain to her that there *was no bomb*?'

We glared angrily at each other. I had won that round. But then he smiled, as if to say he had something better. It was, his smile said, time to pull out the big guns.

'When Rachel North came to one of our meetings in the upstairs room of a pub,' he said, 'I thought her behaviour showed signs of . . .' He paused. 'Mental illness.'

'You think Rachel's *mentally ill*?' I said. It was a low blow.

'It was the degree to which she attacked me,' David said. 'She stood up and came running towards me and shouted at me. There was a *madness* to this—'

'But that's because she thinks it's nonsense—' I interrupted.

'She won't look at the *evidence*,' interrupted David. 'I'm getting the same sort of vibe off you here, Jon. A viewpoint arrived at without evidence is *prejudice*. To say Muslims carried out 7/7 – those three guys from Leeds and one from Aylesbury – to say they did it is *racist*. Jon. It's racist. It's racist. You're being *racist* to Muslims if you think they carried out that attack on the evidence there.'

There was a short silence.

'Oh, *fuck off*,' I said.

That evening I telephoned Rachel to tell her I'd spent the afternoon with David Shayler.

'What did he say?' she asked.

'That you either didn't exist or were mentally ill,' I said.

'It's all because of that stupid meeting,' she said.

'They make it sound like I got up from the floor, marched up onto the stage and started declaiming away. That's not what happened. The whole room erupted in shouting. Everybody started shouting. Yes, I raised my voice to be heard over them shouting. But they shouted. I shouted . . .'

My interview with David Shayler – the 'fuck off' included – was broadcast one night a few weeks later on BBC Radio 4. I began panicking during the hours before it aired. I believe my amygdala went into overdrive. Was I – in telling David Shayler to fuck off – about to open a Pandora's box? Would I incur the wrath of the 7/7 Truth movement? Would they come after me, guns a-blazin', in the same way they had endeavoured to ruin Rachel's life? There was nothing I could do. Wheels were in motion. Somewhere inside some BBC building the tape was stacked up, ready to be broadcast.

For the first few hours the following morning I was too nervous to open my email inbox. But then I did. And it was – I discovered to my delight – filled with congratulations from listeners. The consensus was that I had struck a blow for rational thinking. This felt good: it is always good to be commended for thinking rationally. It became one of my big interviews. It caught the public's imagination. I didn't hear from the July 7th Truth Movement at all. My amygdala went back to normal. Life moved on.

• • •

A few months passed. And then David Shayler was everywhere. He was on BBC Radio 2's *Jeremy Vine Show* and BBC Five Live's *Stephen Nolan* show. There was a double-page spread in the *New Statesman*. The reason was that he had developed an unexpected new theory:

> I ask Shayler if it's true he has become someone who believes that no planes at all were involved in the 9/11 atrocity. [His girlfriend Annie] Machon looks uncomfortable. 'Oh, fuck it, I'm just going to say this,' he tells her. 'Yes, I believe no planes were involved in 9/11.' But we all saw with our own eyes the two planes crash into the WTC. 'The only explanation is that they were missiles surrounded by holograms made to look like planes,' he says. 'Watch the footage frame by frame and you will see a cigar-shaped missile hitting the World Trade Center.' He must notice that my jaw has dropped. 'I know it sounds weird, but this is what I believe.'
>
> – Brendan O'Neill, *New Statesman*,
> September 11th 2006

David Shayler had become part of a rare and extreme faction of the 9/11 Truth Movement – a 'no-planer' – and journalists who would normally find the movement a little too dry to cover were suddenly entranced.

I telephoned him.

'There is no evidence of planes being used apart from a few dodgy witness statements,' he said.

'And . . .' I said.

'And some very obviously doctored footage,' said David.

'But the footage was going out live,' I said.

'Ah, no,' said David. 'The footage was going out on a time delay.'

'Are you in trouble with your girlfriend and the more conservative elements of the Truth movement?' I asked.

I heard David sigh, sadly. 'Yes,' he said. 'They asked me to keep the hologram theory to myself.' He paused. 'Apparently there's going to be a motion in the upcoming Truth movement AGM to disown me.'

I could tell he felt stung, but he said he didn't care. 'Jeremy Vine, Stephen Nolan, this is very prestigious stuff, listened to by millions of people,' he said.

'Jeremy Vine and Stephen Nolan only want you on because your theory sounds *nuts*,' I said.

David countered that not only was it not nuts, but in terms of holograms this was just the beginning. Plans were afoot to 'create the ultimate false flag operation, which is to use holograms to make it look like an alien invasion is underway.'

'Why would they want to do that?' I asked.

'To create martial law across the planet and take away all our rights,' he said.

Actually, the idea that the government may one day utilize holograms to mislead a population was not quite as far-fetched as it sounded. Some years earlier I had come across a leaked US Air Force Academy report entitled *Nonlethal Weapons: Terms and References* which listed all the exotic weapons in the proposal or developmental stages within the US Department of Defense. One section was labelled 'Holograms':

HOLOGRAM, DEATH.
Hologram used to scare a target individual to death. Example, a drug lord with a weak heart sees the ghost of his dead rival appearing at his bedside and dies of fright.

HOLOGRAM, PROPHET.
The projection of the image of an ancient god over an enemy capitol whose public communications have been seized and used against it in a massive psychological operation.

HOLOGRAM, SOLDIERS-FORCES.
The projection of soldier-force images which make an opponent think more allied forces exist than actually do, make an opponent believe that allied forces are located in a region where none actually exist, and/or provide false targets for his weapons to fire upon.

'So maybe David isn't quite as crazy as he seems,' I thought.

A year passed. And then an email arrived:

SEPTEMBER 5TH 2007
Dear All
This is absolutely serious. Please don't miss the

biggest story in history: at the darkest hour, Jesus returns to save humanity. Location of press conference will be Parliament Green, next to the Houses of Parliament and the river at 1400 hours, Thursday 6th September.

Love & Light

Dave Shayler

David was to announce – his attached press release explained – that he was the Messiah.

Journalists are asked to arrive with an open mind as this is a truth which they are in no position to determine and they may be risking their chances of eternal life.

This is all rather embarrassing for someone who was an atheist technocrat three years ago. And I am painfully aware how mad all this sounds. There is however ancient evidence to show that the Messiah is phonetically called 'David Shayler'. When added to recent signs which have appeared independently of me – including a Messianic Cross of Saturn, Mercury, Venus and the Sun in the skies on 7/7/7, the day I was proclaimed Messiah – it has become inescapable that a higher power is indicating that I am the anointed or chosen one who has come to save humanity.

Other incarnations have included Tutenkhamen, King Arthur, Mark Anthony, Leonardo da Vinci, Lawrence of Arabia and Astronges, a Hebrew shepherd and revolutionary leader crucified in Palestine in 1 BC.

David Michael Shayler

It was a surprisingly small turnout. David was sitting in the centre of a circle, dressed in flowing white robes, looking slim and well. There were only two journalists in attendance – someone from Sky News and me. Everyone else seemed to be old friends from the Truth movement. They looked embarrassed.

The man from Sky News told me he was here to interview David but they had no intention to broadcast it. The plan was to get it in the can and then put it on the shelf, 'in case something happens in the future'.

There was no doubting that the 'something' he was alluding to would be something truly awful.

David was telling his cluster of listeners that the signs were there from the beginning.

'Remember when I answered that advert in the *Independent*,' he said, '*Godot Isn't Coming*? I believe it was tailored for me. It even had the word God in the title – *Godot Isn't Coming*.'

'Why would MI5 want to tailor a recruitment advert just for you?' I asked.

'I believe it's MI5's job to protect the incarnations of the Messiah,' he said. 'I know how MI5 works. They want to get in contact with you. They know through tapping your phone that you're looking for a job, you read a certain newspaper. So they'll target an advert at you. Interestingly enough, nobody else was recruited from that ad.'

I got talking to the woman standing next to me. She said her name was Belinda and she'd once been David's landlady. As David continued to preach she whispered to me that she couldn't just sit back and listen any more. It was too sad. She had to say something.

'Uh, David, can I . . .' she began.

'How *dare* you interrupt the Messiah,' David replied.

'OK,' Belinda sighed. 'Carry on.'

'Being the saviour,' David crossly told her, 'I'm *trying* to explain how people can access eternal life . . .'

'All right, sorry . . .' muttered Belinda.

'. . . and people who want to gain eternal life will *probably* want to hear it from me without interruptions . . .' David said. 'I'll take questions at the end, Belinda, but I am trying to tell an important story.'

'I think it's rather a sad story, David,' said Belinda. 'According to Messiah culture, or prophet culture, you're making several mistakes. Firstly, you're not taking time out to really meditate on your mission. You're coming public far too soon. Secondly, you're not gathering a following around you. Thirdly, you're announcing it yourself when really it should be for other people to say, "He is the One," and start to bow down to you or whatever. But you're coming out and throwing it at everybody. My point is, you're not behaving in a very Messiah-like way.'

David shot back that seeing as how he *was* the Messiah *any* way he behaved should be considered a Messiah-like way.

'How are you suddenly an expert on Messiahs?' he snapped.

'I see someone with huge talents and a first-class mind,' said Belinda, 'who was doing extremely well along the track that he was going down, suddenly blowing the whole thing by going off on some esoteric trip.

You're spewing out all sorts of stuff that people just can't connect with other than on the level of ridicule. Which is a terrible shame.'

David looked evenly at her. 'I know I am the Messiah,' he said. 'It's up to you to find out why you can't accept that.'

David spoke a lot during the press conference about the urgent need to get the message out, but during the weeks that followed nothing much happened. There were one or two interviews, but nothing like the number he'd done around the hologram time. I began to see the arc of David Shayler's madness in terms of a graph:

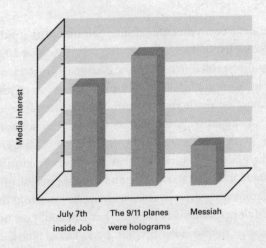

David Shayler's madness

How the arc of David Shayler's madness intersects with media interest.

There seemed to be a tacit consensus that in David's case the 'July 7th never happened' claim was a little too dull to be the right sort of madness, the hologram/plane theory was ideal, and the Messiah was the wrong sort of madness. But why? What made one appropriate and the other not? Most journalists would presumably plead innocence, saying the holograms seemed an innocuous enough cough along the way to the obvious lung cancer of the Messiah declaration – and of course there would be some truth to this – but I wasn't sure it was as simple as that. Both theories seemed to be palpable manifestations of mental illness, yet only one had proved to be a ticket to the airwaves.

For the next two years David dropped out of the public eye completely. The only sighting was in August 2009 when police raided a squat at a National Trust farmhouse in Surrey. Blurry camera-phone footage of the forced eviction made its way onto the Internet. It comprised for the most part squatters yelling, 'I'm not contracting with you,' at the police as they were dragged from their beds. But for a moment amid the commotion the camera whipped to the side and caught glimpse of a very glamorously dressed transvestite. She later told the *Daily Mail* her name was Delores, but you could see under the wig and the make-up that it was David Shayler.

As it happens transvesticism – or Transvestic Fetishism – is, I was surprised to learn while riffling through DSM-IV, a mental disorder:

Usually the male with Transvestic Fetishism keeps a collection of female clothes that he intermittently uses to cross-dress . . . In many or most cases sexual arousal is produced . . . [although] the motivation for cross-dressing may change over time with sexual arousal diminishing or disappearing. In such incidents the cross-dressing becomes an antidote to anxiety or depression or contributes to a sense of peace and calm.

David Shayler, as Delores.

Another year passed during which time I solved the *Being or Nothingness* mystery, met the Scientologists and Tony in Broadmoor, attempted to prove (with mixed results) Bob Hare's theory that psychopaths rule the world, and became uncomfortably conscious of the fact that being a psychopath-spotter had turned me somewhat power-crazed. Actually, I now realized, I had been a somewhat power-crazed madness-spotter for twenty years. It is what we journalists do. It was why I had taken to being a psychopath-spotter with such aplomb. I was good at spotting the diamonds of craziness amid the gloom of normality because it's what I've done for a living for twenty years. There can be something quite psychopathic about journalism, about psychology, about the art of madness-spotting. After I'd met Charlotte Scott I'd consoled myself with the idea that this kind of thing only happened in entertainment-reality TV circles, and I was above it, but the David Shayler story demonstrated that this wasn't true. Political journalism is no different. I was writing a book about the madness industry and only just realizing that I was a part of the industry.

My mind kept returning to the conundrum of why David's hologram theory had proved such a hit with the media yet his Messiah claims went essentially ignored. Why was one the right sort of madness and the other the wrong sort of madness? What was the formula? What did that formula say about us, the journalists and the audience?

I emailed him. Could I pay him one last visit? He replied straight away:

> Jon
> Got your email. Sure thing.

Phone isn't working at the moment. And I'm in Devon. Come and see me and ask whatever you like.

David

It really looked like he'd landed on his feet. It was a lovely cottage in a tiny hamlet. The views from the hot tub on the back porch stretched out across Dartmoor. The cottage had a home cinema and a sauna. David – who was dressed as a man, in a white jumper and leather trousers – looked healthy and happy.

'I live entirely without money,' he said as he made me coffee, 'but I have a fairly good quality of life. I am looked after by God.'

But, it soon became clear, he hadn't landed on his feet at all. He was only staying in this cottage for a few months and the truth was he was destitute. The good nights were when he slept under tarpaulin in an eco-village in Kew, West London. The bad nights were when he slept rough in a town park in some place like Guildford.

The most stable time, he said, was about a year earlier, when he briefly found a new girlfriend, his first since Annie Machon had left him.

'I gave this talk at a retreat and this woman came up to me and said she was the Bride of Christ. I checked it out with God and it turned out that she *was* an incarnation of one of the gods and so I started going out with her.' David paused. 'It turned out to be quite a peculiar relationship.'

'You surprise me,' I said.

'We ended up having a spectacular argument,' he said. 'She had this group around her that worshipped her. I asked the group for permission to dress as Delores, and they said it was fine, but when I did they all turned on me. They started snarling at me, accused me of all sorts of things, like being a tart, weird, perverted, not showing my girlfriend respect. They wouldn't let me leave. And then they threw me out.'

We went up to the attic room, where David had been sleeping these past weeks under a Thomas the Tank Engine duvet. A pile of CCHR DVDs – films produced by Brian's anti-psychiatry branch of the Church of Scientology – sat next to his computer, with titles like *Making a Killing: The Untold Story of Psychotropic Drugging*. David said the Scientologists may be nuts but the DVDs really helped open his eyes.

For a moment the sight of Thomas the Tank Engine made me feel desperately sad, childhood being a halcyon, untroubled time before madness sets in. But, actually, diagnoses of mental disorders in children have mushroomed lately to endemic levels. For instance: when I was a child fewer than one in two thousand children were diagnosed with autism. Now the figure was greater than one in a hundred. When I was driving to the Coxsackie Correctional Facility in upstate New York to meet Toto Constant, I passed a billboard that read EVERY 20 SEC-ONDS A CHILD IS DIAGNOSED WITH AUTISM. The same was true for Childhood Bipolar Disorder. There used to be no diagnoses at all. Now there was an epidemic in America.

• • •

I asked David if the sharp decline in media interest had taken him by surprise. He nodded.

'According to the Bible,' he said, 'I was supposed to spend three days in hell after my crucifixion. Well: I was crucified in September 2007 . . .'

'When you came out as Jesus?' I asked.

'Right,' said David. 'Biblical units are notoriously bad and I think when it said three days in hell it actually meant three *years* in hell.'

'Tell me about the three years in hell,' I said.

'I'm still in them,' David said.

'What do you mean by hell?' I asked.

'Hell is to be a teacher,' David said, 'to have a message you want to get out, but nobody takes a blind bit of notice of you because you say you're Jesus Christ, because God's *telling* you to say it.' He paused. 'God's testing me. He knows I can do that stuff on stage and on the radio and TV. It's part of my test to not be allowed to do what I think I do well. To teach me humility, and so on.' David nodded. 'Yeah,' he said. 'God's testing me. And the test is whether I can continue to believe I'm Christ in the face of the opposition of six billion human beings.'

'When was the last time you talked to God?' I asked.

'We had a short conversation just before you came,' he replied. There was a Hebrew book on the table. 'God told me to open the book for inspiration. I got the page for speaking the right words.'

I picked up the book. It opened randomly to a double page filled with boxes, each containing a few Hebrew letters.

'It's a table of the seventy-two names of God,' David said. 'Look at this . . .'

He pointed haphazardly at a few.

'That translates as David Shayler the Fish,' he said.

He pointed haphazardly at a few more.

'That translates as David Shayler Righteous Chav,' he said.

'David Shayler Righteous Chav?' I said.

'God laughed his head off when He pointed that out to me,' he said. 'It was the first time God and I had ever laughed together.'

I looked down at the table of the seventy-two boxes. 'Surely you're finding a pattern where there are no patterns,' I said.

'Finding patterns is how Intelligence works,' David snapped back. 'It's how research works. It's how journalism works. The search for patterns. Don't you see? That's what *you* do!'

Our conversation turned once again to David's unhappiness at no longer being a popular talk-show guest. He said he found it inexplicable and a real pity.

'A lot of people are scared they're going mad these days,' he said, 'and it's comforting for them to hear someone like me on the radio, someone who has the same "crazy" beliefs they have, about 9/11 and 7/7, but sounds happy, and not mad. I challenge anyone to come and see me and leave believing I sound mad.'

On the drive back to London from Devon it hit me: David was right. A lot of people *are* scared they're going mad. Late at night, after a few drinks, they admit it. One or two of my friends swear they don't mind. One woman I know says she secretly wills a nervous breakdown on so she can get admitted to a psychiatric hospital, away from the tensions of modern life, where she'll be able to have long lie-ins and be looked after by nurses.

But most of my friends do mind, they say. It scares them. They just want to be normal. I'm one of them, forever unpleasurably convinced my wife is dead because I can't reach her on the phone, letting out involuntary yelps on claustrophobic Ryanair flights, becoming debilitatingly anxious that psychopaths might want to kill me. And we spend our evenings watching *Wife Swap* and *Come Dine with Me* and *Supernanny* and the early rounds of *X-Factor* and *Big Brother*. TV is just troubled people being booed these days.

> There's a load of films being made where film-makers go to a council estate and 90% of the people there are functional – getting their kids ready for school, paying their taxes, working. And 10% are dysfunctional – and they go, 'That's what we're going to make a film about.'
> Eddie Marsan, actor. Interviewed by Jonathan Romney in the *Independent*, Sunday, 2 May 2010

Practically every peak-time programme is populated by people who are just the right sort of mad, and I now knew what the formula was. The people who are the right sort of mad are a bit madder than we fear we're becoming, and in a recognizable way. We might be anxious but we aren't as anxious as *them*. We might be paranoid but we aren't as paranoid as *them*.

We are entertained by them, and comforted that we're not as mad as they are.

David Shayler's tragedy is that his madness has spiralled into something too outlandish, too far out of the ball park, and consequently useless. We don't want *obvious* exploitation. We want smoke-and-mirrors exploitation.

But we weren't only in the business of madness, we were also in the business of conformity. I remembered Mary Barnes, the woman in the basement at R. D. Laing's Kingsley Hall who smeared herself in her own shit. Eventually she began smearing paints on canvas instead and became a celebrated artist. London society back in the 1960s and 1970s revered the way her paintings offered a profound glimpse into the insane mind. But Charlotte Scott, and all the other journalists, myself included, weren't scouring the planet for people who possessed the right sort of madness for television so we could *revere* them. When we served up the crazy people, we were showing the public what they *shouldn't* be like. Maybe it was the trying so hard to be normal that was making everyone so afraid they were going crazy.

A few days after I returned from Devon I got a call from Bob Hare.

9

AIMING A BIT HIGH

Bob was spending a Saturday night at Heathrow – a stopover between Sweden and Vancouver, he spends his life crisscrossing the planet teaching people how to use his PCL-R Checklist – and did I want to meet at his hotel for a drink?

When I arrived there was no sign of him in the foyer. The queue for the front desk was long, a lot of tired, unhappy-looking business travellers checking in late. I couldn't see the house phone. Then I had a brainwave. The concierge's desk was unoccupied. His phone was sitting there. I could dial zero, go straight through to the front desk (callers to hotel front desks invariably get to jump the queue: we, as a people, seem more enticed by mysterious callers than we are by actual people standing in front of us) and ask to be put through to Bob's room.

But I only got as far as picking up the phone before I saw the concierge marching fast towards me.

'Put down my phone!' he barked.

'Just give me a second!' I cheerfully mouthed.

He grabbed the phone from my hand and slammed it down.

Bob appeared. I made a big, suave show in front of the concierge of greeting him.

'Bob!' I said.

We were two courteous business travellers meeting for important reasons in a hotel late in the evening. I made sure the concierge saw that.

'Will we go to the third-floor executive bar?' Bob said.

'Yes,' I said, shooting the concierge a glance. 'The executive bar.'

We walked across the lobby together.

'You'll never *believe* what just happened,' I said in a startled whisper.

'What?' said Bob.

'The concierge just manhandled me.'

'In what way?'

'I was using his phone to try and call you and when he saw me he grabbed it out of my hand and slammed it down,' I said. 'It was totally uncalled for and actually quite shocking. Why would he want to *do* that?'

'Well, he's one,' said Bob.

I looked at Bob.

'A *psychopath*?' I said.

I narrowed my eyes and glanced over at the concierge. He was helping someone into the lift with their bags.

'*Is* he?' I said.

'A lot of psychopaths become gatekeepers,' said Bob, 'concierges, security guards, masters of their own domains.'

'He did seem to have a lack of empathy,' I said. 'And poor behavioural controls.'

'You should put *that* in your book,' said Bob.

'I *will*,' I said.

Then I peered at Bob again.

Was that a bit trigger-happy? I thought. Maybe the guy has just had a long, bad day. Maybe he's been ordered by his bosses not to let guests use his phone. Why did neither Bob nor I think about that?

We got the lift to the executive floor.

It was nearly midnight. We drank whisky on the rocks. Other business travellers – those with the key card to the executive bar – typed away on laptops, stared out into the night. I was a little drunk.

'It's quite a power you bestow upon people,' I said. 'The power to spot psychopaths.' Bob shrugged. 'But what if you've created armies of people who've gone power-mad?' I said. 'Who spot psychopaths where there are none, witchfinder-generals of the psychopath-spotting world?'

There was a silence.

'I do worry about the PCL-R being misused,' Bob said. He let out a sigh, stirred the ice around in his drink.

'Who misuses it?' I asked.

'Over here you have your DSPD programme,' he said.

'That's where my friend Tony is,' I said. 'The DSPD unit at Broadmoor.'

'If thirty is the cut-off point, who gives the score?' Bob said. 'Who administers that? Actually, there's a lot of diligence in the UK. But in the US we have the Sexually Violent Predator Civil Commitment stuff. They can apply to have sexual offenders "civilly committed". That means forever . . . .'

Bob was referring to mental hospitals like Coalinga, a pretty 320-acre facility near Monterey Beach, California. The vast hospital (1.2 million square feet) has gyms and music and arts rooms, baseball fields and manicured lawns. 1,500 of California's 100,000 paedophiles are housed there, in comfort, almost certainly until the day they die (only thirteen have ever been released since the place opened in 2005). These 1,500 men were told on the day of their release from jail that they'd been deemed reoffending certainties and were being sent to Coalinga instead of being freed.

'PCL-R plays a role in that,' said Bob. 'I tried to train some of the people who administer it. They were sitting around, twiddling their thumbs, rolling their eyes, doodling, cutting their fingernails – these were people who were going to *use* it.'

A Coalinga psychiatrist, Michael Freer, told the *Los Angeles Times* in 2007 that more than a third of Coalinga 'individuals' (as the inmates there are called) had been misdiagnosed as violent predators, and would in fact pose no threat to the public if released.

'They did their time, and suddenly they are picked up again and shipped off to a state hospital for essentially an indeterminate period of time,' Freer told the newspaper. 'To get out they have to demonstrate that they are no longer a risk, which can be a very high standard. So, yeah, they do have grounds to be very upset.'

In the executive bar, Bob Hare continued. He told me of an alarming world of globetrotting experts, forensic psychologists, criminal-profilers, travelling the planet armed with nothing much more than a Certificate of Attendance, just like the one I had. These people might have influence at parole hearings and death-penalty hearings, in serial-killer incident rooms, and on and on. I think he saw his checklist as something pure – innocent as only science can be – but the humans who administered it as masses of weird prejudices and crazy predispositions.

When I left Bob that night I made the decision to seek out the man responsible for what must surely be the most ill-fated psychopath-hunt in recent history. His name was Paul Britton. Although he had at one time been a renowned criminal-profiler he'd been a lot less conspicuous, even quite reclusive, these past years, ever since he became mired in his profession's most notorious incident.

I spent the next few days leaving messages for him everywhere, although I didn't hold out hope. And then, late in the evening, my telephone rang. It came up as 'Blocked'.

'I'm sorry,' said the voice. 'My name's Paul Britton. I'm aware you've been trying to . . . sorry . . .' He sounded hesitant, self-effacing.

'Will you talk to me about your criminal-profiling days?' I asked.

I heard him sigh at the memory. 'Spending your life literally in the entrails of some poor soul who has been butchered is no way to pass your time,' he said.

(Actually Paul Britton rarely, if ever, spent time literally in someone's entrails: criminal-profilers don't visit crime scenes. The entrails he came into contact with would have been in police photographs, and in his imagination, when he attempted to visualize whichever psychopathic sex murderer he was profiling.)

'Will you talk to me about those days anyway?' I asked.

'There's a new Premier Inn next to Leicester railway station,' he said. 'I can meet you on Thursday at 11 a.m.'

Paul Britton arrived at the Premier Inn wearing a long black coat reminiscent of the kind of dramatic clothing that Fitz – the brilliant fictional criminal-profiler from the TV series *Cracker* – would wear. But I was probably making that connection because it has always been assumed that Fitz was based on him. We ordered coffee and found a table.

I started carefully by asking him about Bob Hare's checklist – 'He's done a marvellous job,' Britton said. 'It really is a valuable tool,' – and then the conversation dried for a moment and he shifted in his chair and said, 'I don't know if I should tell you a little bit about how it all began for me? Is that OK? Sorry! You need to stop me trundling off if I'm being redundant. I won't be remotely offended by that. But may I . . . ?'

'Yes, yes, please do,' I said.

'It all started back in 1984,' he said, 'when a chap called David Baker, one of the finest detectives you could ever come across, visited my office . . .'

1984. A young woman's body had been found on a lane near the NHS hospital where Paul Britton worked as clinical psychologist. She'd been stabbed while walking her dogs. There were no suspects. Criminal-profiling in Britain barely existed back then but some instinct motivated David Baker – the investigating officer – to seek Britton's opinion.

'David is really the father of psychological profiling in the United Kingdom,' Britton said, 'because he came and asked me the question. Do you follow me? If David hadn't come and asked I would have had no reason to get involved.'

He looked at me. It was obvious he wanted me to say, 'Oh, but *you're* the father of criminal-profiling in the United Kingdom.'

I think he wanted to emphasize that there was more to him than the terrible incident.

'Oh, but you're the father of criminal-profiling in the United Kingdom,' I dutifully said.

And so David Baker watched as Britton 'almost unconsciously began asking myself questions' (as he later wrote in his bestselling memoir *The Jigsaw Man*). 'When did he tie her up? How long had she been conscious? How quickly did she die?'

He eventually announced to Baker that the killer would be a sexual psychopath, a young man in his mid-teens to early twenties, lonely and sexually immature, probably living at home with his parents, a manual worker comfortable with knives, and possessing a big collection of violent pornographic magazines and videos.

'It turned out to be entirely correct and they were very quickly able to lay hands on the person responsible,' Britton said. 'A man called Bostock, I think it was.'

Paul Bostock, who did indeed fit Britton's profile, confessed to the murder, and Britton became a celebrity. There were glowing newspaper profiles. The Home Office brought him in to finesse a newly created Offender Profiling Research Unit and asked him to appear in an ITV series called *Murder in Mind*. He said he was reluctant to become a TV celebrity and only agreed after they explained to him that they wanted to be seen to be at the cutting edge of psychological profiling and reminded him that 'everything I'd done was very successful'.

As the months progressed Britton correctly profiled lots more psychopathic sex murderers, almost all of them young men in their mid-teens to early twenties, living alone or at home with their parents and owning a big collection of violent pornography.

'There is a criticism . . .' I began.

'A *criticism of what*?' Britton unexpectedly snapped.

He had been modest, even meek, until that moment and so this sudden lurch in tone came as a surprise.

'That, uh, your profiles were all of almost identical personality types,' I said.

'Oh, well, that's after the event,' he shrugged.

And in fact he did – according to *The Jigsaw Man* – successfully profile some criminals who weren't the archetype: a blackmailer who slipped razor blades into Heinz baby products turned out to be a former police officer, just as he had apparently predicted.

These were the golden days for him. True, the odd unsubstantiated rumour began to surface of occasions when he may have got it wrong. For instance, it was said, a teenage girl had in 1989 walked into a police station in Leeds and claimed to be a 'brood-mare' for some pillars of the community, including the chief constable and the attorney-general, a member of the House of Lords.

'What's a brood-mare?' the baffled policeman asked the girl.

She explained that she was regularly taken to a flat in the student district of Leeds where, in the basement, which had a pentagram painted on the floor, she was impregnated by the chief constable and his fellow Satanic Freemasons and then, later, the foetus would be ripped from her and sacrificed on the altar to Lucifer.

The policeman didn't know which way to turn. Was she a fantasist or an actual brood-mare? Was his boss a Satanic elder or a victim of slander? And so he asked Britton to assess her testimony. He declared she was telling the truth; the police launched an expensive investigation and found nothing. No altar, no coven, no evidence of brood-mare activity of any kind. The case was quietly dropped.

'A brood-mare?' Britton furrowed his brow when I asked him about this rumour.

'Does it ring any bells?' I asked. 'She said the people

in the Satanic cult were high-ranking police officers and they'd impregnate her and rip out the foetus and use it as a sacrifice to Satan?'

'There are a number of cases I've dealt with over the years involving Satanic activity,' Britton replied. 'It's not uncommon. But I don't remember that one.'

If the brood-mare investigation did happen, he could be forgiven for not remembering. The late 1980s and early 1990s were a whirlwind for him. There were media appearances, policemen queuing up to ask his advice on unsolved sex murders, and so on. He was riding high. And then it all fell apart.

On 15 July 1992 a twenty-three-year-old woman, Rachel Nickell, was found murdered on Wimbledon Common. She'd been stabbed forty-nine times in front of her three-year-old son, Alex. The police, as had become customary in cases like this, asked Britton to draw up an offender profile.

'I rubbed my eyes until white stars bounced across the ceiling,' he later wrote in *The Jigsaw Man*, 'I'd been concentrating so hard it was difficult to refocus.' Then he announced that the killer would be a sexual psychopath, a single man, a manual labourer who lived at home with his parents or alone in a bedsit within walking distance of Wimbledon Common and owned a collection of violent pornography.

It is, in retrospect, sort of understandable why they wrongly believed Colin Stagg was the killer. In a terrible twist of fate he looked an awful lot like the witness sketches of the man seen running away from the scene, which, in turn, looked a lot like the actual murderer, Robert Napper. Plus Colin fitted Britton's profile like a hand in a glove, even more snugly in fact than Robert Napper would turn out to. For instance, Colin lived in a bed-sit a short walking distance from the common, whereas Napper lived in Plumstead, seventeen miles away across London. (Nowadays Robert Napper lived three doors down from Tony in the DSPD unit at Broadmoor. Tony told me nobody on the ward liked him much because he was tricky and weird.)

Stagg had previously been cautioned by the police for sunbathing naked on Wimbledon Common and writing an obscene letter to a woman called Julie he'd contacted via a lonely hearts page in *Loot* magazine. A sign on his front door read 'Christians keep away. A pagan dwells here'. Inside was a collection of pornographic magazines and books on the occult.

However, there was no evidence he was in any way sexually deviant. As he writes in his memoir, *Who Really Killed Rachel?*, 'I consider myself to be a perfectly normal person . . . a normal red-blooded male who yearned for the company of women . . . what I really craved was a solid, dependable relationship ultimately leading to marriage and children.'

But yes, he told the police, he'd been walking his dog on Wimbledon Common the day Rachel was murdered, as he did every day.

The police – strongly suspecting they had their killer – asked Britton if he could devise a way to elicit a confession out of Stagg, or eliminate him from their enquiries. And that's when he had his brainwave.

He suggested that a covert officer should make

contact and allow Stagg to befriend them. The police instructed an undercover policewoman – 'Lizzie James' – to write to Stagg, claiming to be a friend of Julie, the lonely heart from *Loot*.

Unlike the prudish Julie, Lizzie would say, she couldn't get Colin's erotic letter out of her mind. To hammer home the hint she added: 'I have an odd taste in music, my favourite record being *Walk On The Wild Side* by Lou Reed.'

Colin, clearly bowled over by this wonderfully unexpected turn of events, responded immediately.

'I'm painfully lonely,' he wrote, asking Lizzie if she'd mind terribly if he could send her some of his sexual fantasies.

Lizzie replied that it would be a treat: 'I'm sure your fantasies hold no bounds and you are as broadminded and uninhibited as me.'

And so Colin wrote back, detailing the two of them making gentle love in a park on a sunny day whilst whispering, 'I love you. I love you so much.' The fantasy ended with Colin tenderly wiping the teardrops that rolled down Lizzie's cheeks.

The police were thrilled. Colin had introduced the location of a *park*.

But Paul Britton advised caution. It would clearly have been better if his fantasy had been less affectionate and more, well, vicious. So, in her next letters, Lizzie upped the ante. Colin mustn't hold back, she wrote, 'because my fantasies hold no bounds and my imagination runs riot. Sometimes this worries me and it would be nice if you have the same unusual dreams as me . . . I want to feel you all powerful and overwhelming so that

I am completely in your power, defenceless and humili-
ated'.

'You need a damn good fucking by a real man,' Colin
gamely replied. 'I am going to make sure you scream in
agony.' He immediately clarified that he wasn't really a
violent person. He was just saying it because it was the
kind of erotic fantasy he gathered she wanted to hear: 'If
you found it offensive I can't apologise enough.' In fact,
he said, it would be brilliant if she would go round to his
flat so he could cook her 'my speciality rice bolognaise
followed by my homemade raspberry mousse'.

Nonetheless, Paul Britton 'noticed distinct elements
of sadism' in Colin's letters.

And on it went. Lizzie sent Colin a series of letters that strongly implied how incredibly fanciable she
thought he was. Colin's responses indicated that he
couldn't believe his luck. This was surely the greatest
thing that had ever happened to him. The only cloud on
his horizon was the incongruous fact that whenever he
suggested taking things to the next level – by perhaps
meeting up and actually having sex – she invariably went
quiet and backed off. He was puzzled, but put it down to
the mysterious ways of womanhood.

Under Britton's direction Lizzie began dropping hints
to Colin that she had a 'dark secret', something 'bad' and
'brilliant' and 'glorious' that she had done in her past,
which aroused in her 'the most exciting emotions'.

Colin replied that he'd love to hear her dark secret
and actually he had one too: the police wrongly believed
he had murdered Rachel Nickell, 'because I am a loner
and I have ancient native beliefs'.

Lizzie responded that she rather wished he *was* the

murderer: 'It would make things easier for me 'cos I've got something to tell you.' It was her 'dark secret'. Maybe they should have a picnic in Hyde Park and she could reveal her dark secret then. Colin replied that he'd be thrilled to have a picnic and hear her dark secret but it was only fair to inform her that he definitely hadn't killed Rachel Nickell. Still, he inelegantly added, perhaps they could have sex and he could yank her head back with a belt as he entered her from behind whilst 'indulging in carnal lusts every five minutes'.

Lizzie's 'dark secret' – as she finally informed Colin in Hyde Park, a large team of undercover officers monitoring their every move – was that when she was a teenager she'd got involved with some 'special people' – *Satanic* people – and when she was with them 'a baby had had its throat cut. And then the baby's blood was put into a cup, and everybody had a drink, and it was the most electrifying atmosphere.' After they drank the baby's blood they killed its mother: 'She was laid out naked and these knives were brought out and this man handed me one of the knives and he asked me to cut the woman's throat, and I did, and then there was this big orgy, and I was with this man, well, this man was the best ever.'

Lizzie looked at Colin and said she could only ever truly love a man who had done a similar thing.

Colin replied, 'I think you're aiming a bit high.'

During the weeks that followed Lizzie persevered: 'The thought of [the killer] is SO exciting. It's a turn-on to think about the man that did it . . . I want someone like the man who did this thing. I want that man . . . If only you had done the Wimbledon Common murder, if only you had killed her, it would be all right.'

'I'm terribly sorry,' Colin sadly replied, 'but I haven't.'

Still, he dutifully sent her increasingly violent sexual fantasies, involving knives and blood, etc., and when Lizzie handed them to Paul Britton he studied it and solemnly informed the police, 'You're looking at someone with a highly deviant sexuality that's present in a very small number of men in the general population. The chances of there being two such men on Wimbledon Common when Rachel was murdered are incredibly small.'

Lizzie tried one last time to elicit a confession out of him. They met in Hyde Park. 'I try to imagine him,' she wistfully said as they ate sandwiches by the Serpentine, 'and the thought of him is so exciting. Perhaps you are that man. I want you to treat me sort of like that man treated her.'

Colin (as he later wrote) started wondering if Lizzie 'might be mentally disturbed'.

'Maybe we should call it a day,' he said forlornly to her.

And at that she stood up, sighed, and stomped away, passing a nearby yellow van filled with police officers.

A few days later Colin was arrested, charged with Rachel Nickell's murder, and spent the next fourteen months in custody, during which time the real murderer, Robert Napper, killed a mother and her four-year-old daughter,

Samantha and Jazmine Bissett, near his home in Plumstead, East London.

'Samantha's body was so horribly mutilated,' Paul Britton told me at the Premier Inn, 'the police photographer assigned to the crime scene opened the duvet Napper had wrapped her in, took the photograph . . .' Britton paused. He stirred his coffee. He gave me a grave look. 'And *never worked again.*'

And this, Britton's look said, was the world they inhabited, the full horror of which innocent civilians like me would never truly understand.

Finally the Colin Stagg case went to the Old Bailey. The judge took one look at it and threw it out. He said the honey trap was 'deceptive conduct of the grossest kind' and 'the notion of a psychological profile being admissible as proof of identity in any circumstances is redolent with considerable danger.'

And with that Britton's reputation, and the reputation of his profession, was ruined.

Nobody emerged from the story well. The policewoman who played Lizzie James disappeared from history in April 2001 when the BBC reported that she'd received £125,000 compensation for trauma and stress. In 2008 Colin Stagg received compensation of £706,000, but that was only after sixteen years of being turned down for every job he ever applied for amid enduring rumours that he had got away with murder. Paul Britton was placed under charge by the British Psychological Society but the case against him was dropped after his lawyer argued that given the passage of time he wouldn't have a fair hearing. He became a pariah in the offender-profiling world.

Now, at the Premier Inn, I said, 'I'd like to talk about Colin Stagg.'

At this, Britton held up his finger, silently riffled through his bag, and handed me a sheet of paper. It took me a moment to understand what I was reading. Then I got it: it was a statement, prepared by him, for anyone who might ever ask that question.

At the very beginning of the Nickell investigation – his statement claimed – he told the Metropolitan Police that the Plumstead rapist (who eventually turned out to be Robert Napper) was their man. But they wouldn't listen.

I looked up from the page.

'Did you really tell them that?' I asked.

Britton nodded. 'I said, "You're looking at the same offender. I met him in Plumstead and I met him at Rachel Nickell." They said, "Our analysis is clear. They're not linked." OK. They're the Metropolitan Police. They know these things. I'm not perfect. It would be arrogant of me to feel that my analysis was superior to theirs. And they're right. It would be. I had to learn it. I had to accept it. Consider this a tutorial. There we are. Sorry.'

'Can you give me proof?' I asked. 'Is there anybody out there who'd be willing to say, "Absolutely yes, this is totally true"?'

'There are a number of people who could say that. None of them will.'

'Because of their vested interests?'

'Because of their pensions and their situation and their interests. But I had a phone call from two people who said, "I was there. I know what happened. You're right. Forgive me for not saying anything. Maybe when I've collected my pension I'll say so." '

'I don't suppose any of them have collected their pensions yet?'

'Folks look after their own lives. You can't blame them. It's rough and tumble . . .'

'Oh,' I said.

He looked at me. 'Let me try and help you with this . . .' he said.

For the next half-hour Britton patiently broke down the events of the honey-trap for me to demonstrate that at no point did he do anything wrong. His rule throughout was that 'the suspect, Colin Stagg, must be the person who introduces every single element. What you may then do is reflect that back. You must never introduce it first. If you do you're fulfilling *your* hopes, you see?'

I was open-mouthed. I didn't know where to start.

'But what about Lizzie's past ritual murders?' I said.

'How . . . sorry . . . what are you thinking there?' Britton softly replied, shooting me a hostile glance.

'She said she could only love a man who'd done something similar,' I said.

'If someone who you were walking out with said that to you,' Britton said, 'what would you do?' He paused and repeated, '*What would you do?*'

'But he was clearly desperate to lose his virginity to her,' I said.

'I don't know the answer to that,' he said.

It was bewildering that Britton really seemed unable

to appreciate how misshapen the honey-trap had been, but just as startling to me was the realization that it was in some ways an extreme version of an impulse that journalists and nonfiction TV makers – and perhaps psychologists and police and lawyers – understand well. They had created an utterly warped, insane version of Colin Stagg by stitching together the maddest aspects of his personality. Only the craziest journalist would go as far as they did but practically everyone goes a *little* way there.

He glared at me. He repeated his position. At no point during the operation did he cross the line.

'Not even when you said that the chance of there being two such "highly sexually deviant" men on Wimbledon Common at the same time was incredibly small?' I asked.

'Well, remember,' he replied, 'Robert Napper was there, Colin Stagg wasn't. Therefore . . . ?'

'Colin Stagg was there that morning,' I said.

'But he wasn't on the Common *at the same time*!' said Britton.

He shot me a victorious look.

'Do you think Colin Stagg has a deviant sexual personality?' I asked.

'I don't know Colin Stagg,' he replied.

There was a frosty silence.

'Are these the questions you came to ask?' he said.

We got the bill.

10

THE AVOIDABLE DEATH
OF REBECCA RILEY

On a balmy evening in April I was invited to a black-tie Scientology banquet at L. Ron Hubbard's old manor house in East Grinstead. We drank champagne on Hubbard's terrace, overlooking uninterrupted acres of English countryside, and then we were led through to the Great Hall where they sat me on the top table, next to Tony Calder, former manager of the Rolling Stones.

The night began with a strange ceremony. The Scientologists who had increased their donations to over £30,000 were invited onto the stage to accept crystal statuettes. They stood there, beaming, in front of a painted panorama of heavenly clouds as the five-hundred-strong audience rose to their feet in applause and the dry ice pumped around them, giving them a kind of mystical glow.

Then Lady Margaret McNair, head of the UK branch of the CCHR, Scientology's anti-psychiatry wing, made a long and quite startling speech detailing the new mental disorders proposed for inclusion in the forthcoming edition of DSM – DSM-V.

'Have you ever honked your horn in anger?' she said. 'Well! You're suffering from Intermittent Explosive Disorder!'

'Yeah!' the audience yelled. 'Congratulations!'

Actually, Intermittent Explosive Disorder is described as 'a behavioral disorder characterized by extreme expressions of anger, often to the point of uncontrollable rage, that are disproportionate to the situation at hand'.

'Then there's Internet Addiction!' she continued. The audience laughed and catcalled.

Actually, Internet Addiction had already been rejected by the DSM-V board. It had been the idea of a Portland, Oregon-based psychiatrist named Jerald Block: 'Internet addiction appears to be a common disorder that merits inclusion in DSM-V,' he wrote in the March 2008 *American Journal of Psychiatry*. 'Negative repercussions include arguments, lying, poor achievement, social isolation, and fatigue.'

But the DSM-V board had disagreed. They said spending too long on the Internet might be considered a symptom of depression, but not a unique disorder. They agreed to mention it in DSM-V's appendix, but everyone knew the appendix was the graveyard of mental disorders.

(I didn't want to admit it to the Scientologists, but I was secretly in favour of Internet Addiction being classified a disorder, as I rather liked the idea of those people who had debated whether I was a shill or stupid being declared insane.)

Lady Margaret continued her list of outrageous proposed mental disorders:

'Ever had a fight with your spouse? Then you're suffering from Relational Disorder!'

'Woo-hoo!' yelled the audience.

'Are you a bit lazy? Then you've got Sluggish Cognitive Tempo Disorder!'

Then there was Binge Eating Disorder, Passive-Aggressive Personality Disorder, Post-Traumatic Embitterment Disorder . . .

Many in the audience were successful local businesspeople, pillars of the community. I had the feeling that the freedom to argue with their wives and pump their horns in anger were freedoms they truly held dear.

I didn't know what to think. There are a lot of ill people out there whose symptoms manifest themselves in odd ways. It seemed untoward for Lady Margaret – for all the anti-psychiatrists, Scientologists or otherwise – to basically dismiss them as sane because it suited their ideology. At what point does querying diagnostic criteria tip over into mocking the unusual symptoms of people in very real distress? The CCHR had once sent around a press release castigating parents for putting their children on medication simply because they were 'picking their noses':

Psychiatrists have labeled everything as a mental illness from nose picking (Rhinotillexomania) to altruism, lottery and playing with 'action dolls.' They market the spurious idea that DSM disorders such as spelling and mathematics disorders and caffeine withdrawal are as legitimate as cancer and diabetes.

Jan Eastgate, president, Citizens Commission on Human Rights International, June 18th 2002

The thing was, parents weren't putting their children on medication for picking their noses. They were putting them on medication for picking them until their facial bones were exposed.

But as her list continued it was hard not to wonder how things had ended up this way. It really did seem that she was on to something, that complicated human behaviour was increasingly getting labelled a mental disorder. How did this come to be? Did it matter? Were there consequences?

The answer to the first question turned out to be strikingly simple. It was all because of one man in the 1970s: Robert Spitzer.

'For as long as I can remember I've enjoyed classifying people.'

In a large, airy house in a leafy suburb of Princeton, New Jersey, Robert Spitzer – who is in his eighties now and suffering from Parkinson's disease but still very alert and charismatic – sat with his housekeeper and me, remembering his childhood camping trips to upstate New York.

'I'd sit in the tent, looking out, writing notes about

the lady campers,' he said. 'What I thought about each. Their attributes. Which ones I was more taken with.' He smiled. 'I've always liked to classify things. Still do.'

His camping trips were a respite from his tense home life, the result of a 'chronic psychiatric outpatient mother. She was a very unhappy lady. And she was well into psychoanalysis. She went from one analyst to another.'

And she never got better. She lived unhappy and she died unhappy. Spitzer watched this. The psychoanalysts were useless, flailing around. They did nothing for her.

He grew up to be a psychiatrist at Columbia University, his dislike of psychoanalysis remaining undimmed. And then, in 1973, an opportunity to change everything presented itself.

David Rosenhan was a psychologist from Swarthmore College, Pennsylvania, and Princeton. Like Spitzer he'd grown tired of the pseudoscientific, ivory-tower world of the psychoanalyst. He wanted to demonstrate that they were as useless as they were idolized, and so he devised an experiment. He co-opted seven friends, none of whom had ever had any psychiatric problems. They gave themselves pseudonyms and fake occupations and then, all at once, they travelled across America, each to a different mental hospital. As Rosenhan later wrote,

> They were located in five different states on the East and West coasts. Some were old and shabby, some were quite new. Some had good staff–

patient ratios, others were quite understaffed. Only one was a strict private hospital. All of the others were supported by state or federal funds or, in one instance, by university funds.

At an agreed time, each told the duty psychiatrist that they were hearing a voice in their head that said the words 'Empty', 'Hollow' and 'Thud'. That was the only lie they would be allowed to tell. Otherwise they had to behave completely normally.

All eight were immediately diagnosed as insane and admitted into the hospitals. Seven were told they had schizophrenia, one manic depression.

Rosenhan had expected the experiment would last a couple of days. That's what he'd told his family: that they shouldn't worry and he'd see them in a couple of days. They didn't let him out for two months.

In fact they refused to let any of the eight out, for an average of nineteen days each, even though they all acted completely normally from the moment they were admitted. When staff asked them how they were feeling they said they were feeling fine. They were all given powerful anti-psychotic drugs.

Each was told that he would have to get out by his own devices, essentially by convincing the staff that he was sane.

Simply telling the staff they were sane wasn't going to cut it.

Once labeled schizophrenic the pseudopatient
was stuck with that label.
— David Rosenhan, *On Being Sane In Insane
Places*, 1973

There was only one way out. They had to agree with
the psychiatrists that they were insane and then pretend
to get better.

When Rosenhan reported the experiment there was
pandemonium. He was accused of trickery. He and
his friends had faked mental illness! You can't blame a
psychiatrist for misdiagnosing someone who presented
himself with fake symptoms! One mental hospital chal-
lenged Rosenhan to send some more fakes, guaranteeing
they'd spot them this time. Rosenhan agreed, and after a
month the hospital proudly announced they had discovered forty-one fakes. Rosenhan then revealed he'd sent
no one to the hospital.

The Rosenhan experiment was a disaster for American
psychiatry. Robert Spitzer was delighted.

'It was very embarrassing,' he said to me now.
'The self-esteem of psychiatry got very low as a result
of it. It had never really been accepted as part of
medicine because the diagnoses were so unreliable, and
the Rosenhan experiment confirmed it.'

Spitzer's respect lay instead with psychologists like
Bob Hare who eschewed psychoanalysis for something
more scientific — checklists — emotionless catalogues of

overt behaviour. If there was only some way of bringing that kind of discipline into psychiatry.

Then he heard there was a job going, editing the new edition of a little-known spiral-bound booklet called DSM.

'The first edition of DSM had been sixty-five pages!' Spitzer laughed. 'It was mainly used for state hospitals reporting on statistics. It was of no interest to researchers at all.'

He happened to know some of the DSM people. He'd been around when gay activists had lobbied them to get the mental disorder of Homosexuality removed. Spitzer had been on the activists' side and had brokered a deal that meant being gay was no longer a manifestation of insanity. His intervention gained him respect from everyone and so when he expressed interest in the job editing DSM-III, it was a foregone conclusion.

'Anyway,' he said, 'there was nobody vying for the job. It wasn't regarded as a very important job.'

What nobody knew was that Spitzer had a plan – to remove, as much as he could, human judgement from psychiatry.

For the next six years, from 1974 to 1980, he held a series of DSM-III editorial meetings inside a small conference room at Columbia University. They were, by all accounts, chaos. As the *New Yorker*'s Alix Spiegel later reported, the psychiatrists Spitzer invited would yell over each other. The person with the loudest voice tended to get taken the most seriously. Nobody took minutes.

'Of course we didn't take minutes,' Spitzer told me. 'We barely had a typewriter.'

Someone would yell out the name of a potential new mental disorder and a checklist of its overt characteristics, there'd be a cacophony of voices in assent or dissent, and if Spitzer agreed, which he almost always did, he'd hammer it out then and there on an old typewriter, and there it would be, sealed in stone.

It seemed a foolproof plan. He would eradicate from psychiatry all that crass sleuthing around the unconscious. There'd be no more silly polemicizing. Human judgement hadn't helped his mother. Instead it would be like science. Any psychiatrist could pick up the manual they were creating – DSM-III – and if the patient's overt symptoms tallied with the checklist they'd get the diagnosis.

And that's how practically every disorder you've ever heard or have been diagnosed with came to be invented, inside that chaotic conference room, under the auspices of Robert Spitzer, who was taking his inspiration from checklist pioneers like Bob Hare.

'Give me some examples,' I asked him.

'Oh . . .' He waved his arm in the air to say there were just so many. 'Post-Traumatic Stress Disorder. Borderline Personality Disorder, Attention Deficit Disorder . . .'

Then there was Autism, Anorexia Nervosa, Bulimia, Panic Disorder . . . every one a brand-new disorder with its own checklist of symptoms.

Here, for instance, is part of the checklist for Bipolar Disorder from DSM-IV:

CRITERIA FOR MANIC EPISODE
    A distinct period of abnormally and persistently elevated, expansive or irritable mood lasting at least one week.

Inflated self-esteem and grandiosity.

Decreased need for sleep (e.g., feels rested after only 3 hours of sleep).

More talkative than usual or pressure to keep talking.

Excessive involvement in pleasurable activities that have a high potential for painful consequences (e.g., engaging in unrestrained buying sprees, sexual indiscretions, or foolish business investments).

WITH MELANCHOLIC FEATURES

Loss of pleasure in all, or almost all, activities.

Lack of reactivity to usually pleasurable stimuli (does not feel much better, even temporarily, when something good happens).

Excessive or inappropriate guilt.

Problems include school truancy, school failure, occupational failure, divorce, or episodic anti-social behavior.

'Were there any proposals for mental disorders you rejected?' I asked Spitzer.

He thought for a moment.

'Yes,' he finally said. 'I do remember one. Atypical Child Syndrome.'

There was a short silence.

'Atypical Child Syndrome?' I said.

'The problem was when we tried to find out how to characterize it. I said, "What are the symptoms?" The man proposing it replied, "That's hard to say because the children are very atypical." ' He paused. 'And we were going to include Masochistic Personality Disorder, but there were a bunch of feminists who were violently opposed.'

'Why?'

'They thought it was labelling the victim.'

'What happened to it?'

'We changed the name to Self Defeating Personality Disorder and put it into the appendix.'

I'd always wondered why there had been no mention of psychopaths in the DSM. It turned out, Spitzer told me, that there had indeed been a backstage schism – between Bob Hare and a sociologist named Lee Robins. She believed clinicians couldn't reliably measure personality traits like empathy. She proposed dropping them from the DSM checklist and only going for overt symptoms. Bob vehemently disagreed, the DSM committee sided with Lee Robins, and Psychopathy was abandoned for Antisocial Personality Disorder.

'Robert Hare is probably quite annoyed with us,' Spitzer said.

'I think so,' I said. 'I think he feels you plagiarized his criteria without crediting him.'

(I later heard that Bob Hare might get his credit after all. A member of the DSM-V steering committee, David Shaffer, told me they were thinking of changing the name of Antisocial Personality Disorder – it sounds so damning – and someone suggested calling it Hare Syndrome. They're mulling it.)

• • •

In 1980, after six years inside Columbia, Spitzer felt ready to publish. But first he wanted to road-test his new checklists. And there were a lot. DSM-I had been a sixty-five-page booklet. DSM-II was a little longer – 134 pages. But DSM-III, Spitzer's DSM, was coming in at 494 pages. He turned the checklists into interview questionnaires and sent researchers out into America to ask hundreds of thousands of people at random how they felt.

It turned out that almost all of them felt terrible. And according to the new checklists, more than 50 per cent of them were suffering from a mental disorder.

DSM-III was a sensation. Along with its revised edition, it sold more than a million copies. Sales to civilians hugely outweighed sales to professionals. Many more copies were sold than psychiatrists existed. All over the Western world people began using the checklists to diagnose themselves. For many of them it was a godsend. Something was categorically wrong with them and finally their suffering had a name. It was truly a revolution in psychiatry, and a gold rush for drug companies who suddenly had hundreds of new disorders they could invent medications for, millions of new patients they could treat.

'The pharmaceuticals were delighted with DSM,' Spitzer told me, and this in turn delighted him: 'I love to hear examples of parents who say, "It was impossible to live with him until we gave him medication and then it was night and day." That's good news for a DSM person.'

But then something began to go wrong.

Gary Meier – the psychiatrist who invented the dream workshops and the chanting rituals at Oak Ridge and was eventually fired for giving LSD to twenty-six psychopaths simultaneously – was recently invited for lunch by some drug company reps. He now works at two maximum-security prisons in Madison, Wisconsin, and his department had just made the decision to have nothing more to do with the drug companies. So a few of the reps invited him for lunch to find out why.

'It was two beautiful women and a pretty nice guy,' Gary told me after the lunch was over.

'What did they say?' I asked him.

'Well, if you look for me on the Internet you'll find essays I've written about Indian effigy mounds,' he replied. 'They're my hobby. So the two beautiful women spent most of the lunch asking me about effigy mounds. They had me drawing pictures of effigies on the tablecloth.'

'And then what?' I asked.

'Then they got down to it,' he said. 'Why wasn't I using their products? I said, "You guys are the enemy. You've hijacked the profession. You're only interested in selling your products, not in treating patients." They all had a run at me. I held my ground. Then the bill came. We were ready to go. And then the more attractive of the two women said, "Oh! Would you like some Viagra samples?" '

Gary fell silent. Then he said, with some fury, 'Like street pushers.'

Gary said he has nothing against checklists: 'A good checklist is useful. But now we're flooded with checklists. You can read them in *Parade* magazine.'

And a surfeit of checklists coupled with unscrupulous drug reps is, Gary said, a dreadful combination.

There is a children's picture book called *Brandon and the Bipolar Bear*, written by a woman named Tracy Anglada. In it, little Brandon flies into a rage at the slightest provocation. At other times he's silly and giddy. His mother takes him and his bear to a doctor, who tells him he has bipolar disorder. Brandon asks the doctor if he'll ever feel better. The doctor says yes, there are now good medicines to help boys and girls with bipolar disorder and Brandon can start by taking one right away. He asks Brandon to promise that he'll take his medicine whenever he's told to by his mother.

Were Brandon an actual child he would almost certainly have just been misdiagnosed with bipolar disorder.

'The USA over-diagnoses many things and childhood bipolar is the latest but perhaps the most worrying given the implications.'

Ian Goodyer is a professor of child and adolescent psychiatry at Cambridge University. He – like practically every neurologist and child psychiatrist operating outside the US, and a great many within the US – simply doesn't believe that childhood bipolar disorder exists.

'Epidemiological studies never find anything like the prevalence quoted by the protagonists of this view that there are bipolar children,' he told me. 'It is an illness that emerges from late adolescence. It is very, very unlikely indeed that you'll find it in children under seven years of age.'

Which is odd, given that huge numbers of American children under seven are currently being diagnosed with it.

These children may be ill, some very ill, some very troubled, Ian Goodyer said, but they are not bipolar.

When Robert Spitzer stepped down as editor of DSM-III his position was taken by a psychiatrist named Allen Frances. He continued the Spitzer tradition of welcoming as many new mental disorders, with their corresponding checklists, into the fold as he could. DSM-IV came in at 886 pages.

Now, as he took a road-trip from New York down to Florida, Dr Frances told me over the phone he felt they'd made some terrible mistakes.

'It's very easy to set off a false epidemic in psychiatry,' he said. 'And we inadvertently contributed to three that are ongoing now.'

'Which are they?' I asked.

'Autism, attention deficit, and childhood bipolar,' he said.

'How did you do it?' I asked.

'With autism it was mostly adding Asperger's, which was a much milder form,' he said. 'The rates of diagnosis of autistic disorder in children went from less than one in two thousand to more than one in one hundred. Many kids who would have been called eccentric, different, were suddenly labelled autistic.'

I remembered my drive to Coxsackie Correctional Facility, passing that billboard near Albany – EVERY 20 SECONDS A CHILD IS DIAGNOSED WITH AUTISM.

Some parents came to wrongly believe that this sudden, startling outbreak was linked to the MMR vaccine. Doctors like Andrew Wakefield and celebrities like Jenny McCarthy and Jim Carrey promoted the view. Parents stopped giving the vaccine to their children. Some caught measles and died.

But this chaos, Allen Frances said, pales next to childhood bipolar.

'The way the diagnosis is being made in America was not something we intended,' he said. 'Kids with extreme irritability and moodiness and temper tantrums are being called bipolar. The drug companies and the advocacy groups have a tremendous influence in propagating the epidemic.'

As it happens, Tracy Anglada, author of *Brandon and the Bipolar Bear*, is the head of a childhood bipolar advocacy group called BP Children. She emailed me that she wished me all the best with my project but she didn't want to be interviewed. If, however, I wanted to submit a completed manuscript to her (she added) she'd be happy to consider it for review.

• • •

'Psychiatric diagnoses are getting closer and closer to the boundary of normal,' said Allen Frances. 'That boundary is very populous. The most crowded boundary is the boundary with normal.'

'Why?' I asked.

'There's a societal push for conformity in all ways,' he said, 'there's less tolerance of difference. And so maybe for some people having a label is better. It can confer a sense of hope and direction. "Previously I was laughed at, I was picked on, no one liked me, but now I can talk to fellow bipolar sufferers on the Internet and no longer feel alone." ' He paused. 'In the old days some of them may have been given a more stigmatizing label like conduct disorder or personality disorder or oppositional defiant disorder. Childhood bipolar takes the edge of guilt away from parents that maybe they created an oppositional child.'

'So maybe it's all good,' I said. 'Maybe being given a diagnosis of childhood bipolar is good.'

'No,' he said. 'It is definitely not good. And there's a very good reason why it isn't.'

Bryna Hebert, who lives two hundred miles from Robert Spitzer in Barrington, Rhode Island, was 'such a high-energy child, would I have been labeled? Probably. I did all kinds of crazy things. Back-flips down the stairs . . .'

But her childhood occurred before DSM-III was published and her behaviour was considered just being a child.

All that changed with her children. I was sitting

with them all in her airy middle-class home. Matt, who was fourteen, wandered around playing 'Smoke on the Water' on a Gibson Epiphone. Hannah worried about whether some leftover food she'd eaten was too old. Jessica wasn't home from school. Everything seemed nice and normal to me. But, then again, Matt was medicated. I visited Bryna because, like her friend Tracy Anglada, she had written a children's book about the condition: *My Bipolar, Roller Coaster, Feelings Book*.

'They were always very high energy,' said Bryna. 'They were difficult kids. They had colic. They had to move. They crawled at six months. They walked at ten months. I'd pick them up from school and the teacher would say, "Hannah had the rice from the rice table today. She filled her mouth with rice from the rice table!" '

Bryna laughed and blushed. She was still a high-energy person – a fast talker, her words and thoughts tumbling out of her.

'We used to have to duct-tape their diapers. They would take them off while they were sleeping. They were pretty high end. Matt! Will you take your medicines please?'

They were lined up on the kitchen table. He took them straight away.

Their nickname for baby Matt was Mr Manic Depressive.

'Because his mood would change so fast. He'd be sitting in his high-chair, happy as a clam, two seconds later he'd be throwing things across the room. He's crying and he's angry and nobody knows why. When he was three he got a lot more challenging. Kids liked him but they were becoming afraid of him because they couldn't predict what he'd do next. He'd hit and not be sorry that he hit. He was obsessed with vampires. He'd cut out bits of paper and put them into his teeth like vampire teeth and go around. Hiss hiss hiss. Walking down the street! Going up to strangers. It was a little weird.'

'Were you getting nervous?' I asked.

'Yeah,' said Bryna. 'We'd get in the car and he'd say he could see the buildings downtown. But they'd be thirty miles away! When he played Lion King he really *was* Simba. He was manic. Not too often depressed. Occasionally. He'd say he didn't deserve to live, but he was never suicidal. And he would have these tantrums that would last a very long time. At home one day he wanted some pretzels before lunch, and I was making lunch, and so I *told* him no. I told him he *couldn't* have the pretzels. And he grabbed a butcher knife and threatened me with the butcher knife. I yelled at him. *Put that down.*'

'How old was he?'

'Four.'

'And did he put it down?'

'Yes.'

'Was that the only time?' I asked.

'That was the only time he's ever done anything that extreme,' said Bryna. 'Oh, he's hit Jessica in the head and kicked her in the stomach.'

'She's the one who punched *me* in the head,' called Matt from across the room.

Bryna looked furious. She calmed herself.

It was after the butcher-knife incident, she said, they took him to be tested.

As it happened, the paediatric unit at their local hospital – Massachusetts General – was run by Dr Joseph Biederman, the doyen of childhood bipolar disorder.

> The science of children's psychiatric medications is so primitive and Biederman's influence so great that when he merely mentions a drug during a presentation, tens of thousands of children within a year or two will end up taking that drug, or combination of drugs. This happens in the absence of a drug trial of any kind – instead, the decision is based upon word of mouth among the 7,000 child psychiatrists in America.
> – *San Francisco Chronicle*, July 13th 2008

In November 2008, Biederman was accused of conflict of interest when it was discovered that his unit had received funding from Johnson & Johnson, maker of the antipsychotic drug Risperdal, which is frequently given to children. Although the hospital denied the unit was promoting Johnson & Johnson products, the *New York Times* published excerpts of an internal document in which Biederman promised to try and 'move forward the commercial goals of J&J'.

Biederman has said that bipolar disorder can start 'from the moment the child opens his eyes.'

He's denied the allegations made against him.

'When they were testing Matt he was turning on the PA system,' said Bryna, 'he was turning off the PA system. He was turning on the lights, he was turning off the lights. He was under the table, he was on top of the table. We went through all these checklists. He said he once had a dream that a big flying bird with rotor blades cut his sister's head off. In another dream he was swallowed up by a ghost. When they heard the dreams they really began to pay attention.'

After a while one of Dr Biederman's colleagues said, 'We really think Matt meets the criteria in the DSM for bipolar disorder.'

That was ten years ago and Matt has been medicated ever since. So has his sister Jessica, who was also diagnosed by Dr Biederman's people as bipolar.

'We've been through a million medications,' said Bryna. 'With the first one he got so much better but he gained ten pounds in a month. So there's weight gain. Tics. Irritability. Sedation. They work for a couple of years then they stop working. MATT!'

Matt was playing 'Smoke on the Water' quite close to us.

'Matt,' she said. 'Will you do this somewhere else? Honey, can you find something to do? Go to another place.'

Bryna is convinced her children are bipolar, and I wasn't going to swoop into a stranger's home for an afternoon and tell them all they were normal. That would be incredibly patronizing and offensive. Plus as David Shaffer – the venerable child psychiatrist, DSM pioneer, and recently separated husband of *Vogue* editor Anna

Wintour – told me when I met him in New York later that evening, 'These kids that are getting misdiagnosed with bipolar can be very oppositional, very disturbed, they're not normal kids. They're very difficult to control and they terrorize and can break up a home. They are powerful kids who can take years off your happy life. But they aren't bipolar.'

'So what are they?' I said.

'ADD?' he said. 'Often when you're with an ADD kid you think, "My God, they're just like a manic adult." Kids with ADD are often irritable. They're often manic. But they don't grow up manic. And manic adults weren't ADD when they were children. But they're being labelled bipolar. That's an enormous label that's going to stay with you for the rest of your life. If you're a girl you're going to have to take medication that can induce all sorts of ovarian disorders, cause significant changes to your metabolic balance. There are the implications of you being told you have a familial genetic condition, which is going to make you unreliable, unpredictable, prone to terrible depressions, prone to suicide . . .'

Bryna works at day-care centres. 'Recently one kid, a foster kid, came in,' she said. 'He had been removed from his home for abuse and neglect. And because he had sexualized behaviours, and because he'd been through some moody stuff, somebody said he had bipolar disorder. He fulfilled the bipolar checklist. See? And so they gave him some pretty heavy-duty medication. It slowed him way down, to a drooling fat kid. And they declared the meds a success.'

It eventually became clear that the boy wasn't bipolar, Bryna said. He was moody and had sexualized behaviour because he had been sexually abused. But they were in thrall to the checklist. His overt symptoms tallied with the traits listed on the checklist. This was one random child in a random day-care centre. A million children have these past few years been diagnosed as bipolar in America.

'Has anyone studied whether bipolar children still get the diagnosis when they reach adolescence?' I asked Bryna.

'Yeah,' she said. 'Some do. Others outgrow it.'

'Outgrow it?' I said. 'Isn't bipolar considered to be lifelong? Isn't that another way of saying they didn't have it to begin with?'

Bryna shot me a sharp look. 'My husband grew out of his asthma and food allergies,' she said.

When I asked Robert Spitzer about the possibility that he'd inadvertently created a world in which some ordinary behaviours were being labelled mental disorders, he fell silent. I waited for him to answer. But the silence lasted three minutes. Finally he said, 'I don't know.'

'Do you ever think about it?' I asked him.

'I guess the answer is I don't really,' he said. 'Maybe I should. But I don't like the idea of speculating how many of the DSM-III categories are describing normal behaviour.'

'Why don't you like speculating on that?' I asked.

'Because then I'd be speculating on how much of it is a mistake,' he said.

There was another long silence.

'Some of it may be,' he said.

On the night of 13 December 2006, in Boston, Massachusetts, Rebecca Riley had a cold and couldn't sleep, and so she called to her mother, who brought her in, gave her some cold medicine, and some of her bipolar medication, and told her she could sleep on the floor next to the bed. When her mother tried to wake her the next morning she discovered her daughter was dead.

The autopsy revealed that her parents had given her an overdose of the anti-psychotic drugs she'd been proscribed for her bipolar disorder, none of which had been approved for use in children. They'd got into the habit of feeding her the pills to shut her up when she was being annoying. They were both convicted of Rebecca's murder.

Rebecca had been diagnosed as bipolar and given medication – ten pills a day – by an upstanding psychiatrist named Dr Kayoko Kifuji, who worked at the Tufts Medical Center and was a fan of Dr Joseph Biederman's research into childhood bipolar. Rebecca had scored high on the DSM checklist, even though she was only three, and like all three-year-olds could barely string a sentence together.

Shortly before her conviction, Rebecca's mother Carolyn was interviewed by CBS's Katie Couric.

KATIE COURIC: Do you think Rebecca really had bipolar disorder?

CAROLYN RILEY: Probably not.

KATIE COURIC: What do you think was wrong
  with her now?
CAROLYN RILEY: I don't know. Maybe she was
  just hyper for her age.

266

11

GOOD LUCK

Two years had passed since Deborah Talmi slid her copy of that mysterious, strange, slim book across the table at the Costa Coffee. Tony from Broadmoor called. I hadn't heard from him in months.

'Jon!' he said. He sounded excited. His excitement sounded like it was echoing down some long, empty corridor.

I was definitely pleased to hear from him although I wasn't sure how pleased it was appropriate for me to be. Who was Tony? Was he Toto Constant, who had struck me as the archetypal Bob Hare psychopath, charming and dangerous, conforming to the checklist with an uncanny, eerie precision? Was he Al Dunlap, who had, I felt in retrospect, been a bit shoehorned by me into the checklist, even if he had himself laid claim to many of the items, seeing them as manifestations of the American Dream, the entrepreneurial spirit? Was he David Shayler, his insanity palpable but harmless to other people, reduced to a plaything for the benefit of the madness industry? Or was he Rebecca Riley or Colin Stagg, wrongly judged insane because they just weren't what the people around them wanted them to be? They were just too difficult, just not normal enough.

'There's going to be a tribunal,' Tony said. 'I want you to come. As my guest.'

'Ah,' I said, trying to sound pleased for him.

Brian, the Scientologist from the CCHR, had told me about Tony's various tribunals. Tony was forever pushing for them, year after year, for the fourteen years he had now been inside Broadmoor's Dangerous and Severe Personality Disorder unit. His optimism was tireless. He'd try and co-opt anyone he could to his side: psychiatrists, Scientologists, me, anyone. But the outcome was always the same. They'd come to nothing.

'Where's the tribunal happening?' I asked.

'Right here,' Tony said. 'Just down the corridor.'

Journalists hardly ever made it to a DSPD unit – my meetings with Tony had always been in the main canteen, the Wellness Centre – and I was curious to see inside. According to Professor Maden, the chief clinician there, it wouldn't exist without Bob Hare's psychopath checklist. Tony was there because he scored high on it, as had all three hundred DSPD patients, including the famous ones like Robert Napper, the man who killed Rachel Nickell on Wimbledon Common, and Peter Sutcliffe, the Yorkshire Ripper, and so on. Britain had five DSPD units – four for men and one, in Durham, for women.

That one was called the Primrose. Tony's was called the Paddock.

The official line was that these were places to treat psychopaths (with cognitive behavioural therapy and anti-libidinous drugs – chemical castrations – for the sexual ones), to teach them how to manage their psychopathy with a view to one day theoretically sending them back out into the world as safe and productive people. But the widespread theory was the whole thing was in fact a scheme to keep psychopaths locked up for life.

'They're just a scam,' Brian had told me when I'd first met him for lunch, some two years earlier. 'Give the prisoners – sorry, the *patients* – some CBT. Define some casual conversation over lunch between a nurse and a patient as therapy. If the patient chats back they're engaging with the therapy. They're being *treated*. That way anyone who scores high on the Hare checklist can be locked up forever.'

The DSPD story began on a summer's day in 1996. Lin Russell and her two daughters, Megan and Josie, and their dog, Lucy, were walking down a country lane when they saw a man watching them from his car. He climbed out and asked them for money. He was holding a hammer.

Lin said, 'I've got no money. Shall I go back in my house and get some?'

The man said, 'No,' and then he started beating them to death. Josie was the only survivor.

The killer's name was Michael Stone and he was a known psychopath. He had previous convictions. But the law stated that only patients whose mental disorders were considered treatable could be detained beyond their prison sentences. Psychopaths were considered untreatable and so Michael Stone had to be free.

After his conviction for the Russell murders the government decided to set up a series of treatment centres – ' "treatment" centres,' Brian said, doing that quotation mark thing with his fingers – for psychopaths. Soon afterwards the DSPD units were built. And indeed, during the ten years that followed, hardly anybody was ever released from one. Once you were a DSPD patient there seemed no way out.

'Oh, by the way,' said Tony on the phone to me now. 'There's something I've been meaning to ask you. A favour.'

'Oh yes?' I said.

'When you write about me in your book,' he said, 'please name me. My real name. None of that stupid "Tony" business. My *real* name.'

The Paddock Centre was a clean, bland, modern, calmingly pine-coloured fortress, a secure unit inside a secure unit. The lighting was glaringly, purposefully bright, eliminating any possibility of shadow. The walls were a pastel yellow, a colour so innocuous it barely existed. The only flashes of anything like an actual colour here were the bold reds of the many panic buttons. They lined the walls at exact intervals. The central heating sounded like a long, loud sigh.

A security guard sat me on a plastic chair in a dull corridor – it was like a brand-new Travel Inn corridor – underneath a panic button.

'Don't worry,' he said, although I hadn't asked, 'no patients can get into this part.'

'Where are the patients?' I asked him.

He nodded towards the end of the corridor. There was a kind of observation room. Beyond it, behind thick clear glass, lay two large, clean, featureless, open-plan wards. A few men shuffled around inside them, the psychopaths, eating chocolates, looking out of the windows at the rolling hills beyond. Somewhere in the near distance, through the snow, lay Windsor Castle, Ascot racecourse, Legoland.

An hour passed slowly. Nurses and security guards came over to say hello and ask me who I was. I said I was a friend of Tony's.

'Oh, Tony,' said one nurse. 'I know Tony.'

'What do you think of Tony?' I asked him.

'I do have strong thoughts about Tony,' he said. 'But it would not be appropriate for me to tell you what they are.'

'Are your thoughts about Tony strongly positive or strongly negative?' I asked.

He looked at me as if to say, 'I am not telling you.'

More time passed. There were four of us in the corridor now: me, the nurse, and two security guards. Nobody said anything.

'I feel quite privileged to be in this building,' I said, breaking the silence.

'Really?' the others said in unison, giving me puzzled looks.

'Well,' I said. 'It's mysterious.' I paused. 'Outsiders don't get to see inside here.'

'We've got some spare beds, if you like,' said the nurse.

And then, suddenly, there was activity. People were coming and going – lawyers, nurses, psychiatrists, magistrates, security guards – all in a big rush, having private, huddled chats, hurrying off to make frantic calls, going off into private rooms together.

'Is it always this busy?' I asked a guard.

'No,' he said. He looked surprised. He sat upright in his chair. 'This isn't normal. Something's happening.'

'Something to do with Tony?' I asked.

'I don't know,' he said. His eyes darted up and down the corridor like a meerkat's. But nobody called upon him to help out with whatever big thing was unfolding, so he slumped back into his chair.

A man stopped to introduce himself. 'I'm Anthony Maden,' he said.

'Oh, hi,' I said. Even though I'd been exchanging emails with him on and off for two years, this was the first time I'd met Tony's clinician, the chief clinician here at the DSPD. He looked younger than I imagined he would, a little scruffier, nicer.

'It's a rollercoaster morning,' he said.

'Because of Tony?' I said.

'All will possibly become clear, or possibly not clear, as the morning progresses,' he said. He started to dash away.

'Oh,' I called after him. 'Tony wants me to name him in my book. His actual name.'

He stopped. 'Ah,' he said.

'But what if he does, finally, get out some time in the future,' I say, 'and some prospective employer reads my book? How will that help him? If the world finds out he's spent half his life in the Dangerous and Severe Personality Disorder Unit at Broadmoor?'

'Quite,' said Anthony Maden.

I lowered my voice. 'I'm a bit worried,' I said, 'that he only wants me to name him because of Item 2 on the Hare Checklist. *Grandiose sense of self-worth.*'

His face brightened as if to say, 'So you *do* understand.'

'Exactly,' he said.

A nice-looking elderly man stopped. He was wearing a tweed suit with a bow tie. 'And who are you?' he asked me.

'I'm a journalist,' I said, 'I'm writing about Tony.'

'Oh, he's a very interesting case,' he said. 'I'm one of the tribunal's magistrates.'

'I think he's interesting too,' I said. 'Professor Maden has always been a bit mystified as to why I want to write about Tony and not, you know, the Stockwell Strangler or someone. But he *is* interesting, isn't he?' I paused. 'So *ambiguous!*'

The magistrate looked at me, his face suddenly darkening. 'You're not a Scientologist, are you?' he asked.

Members of the CCHR frequently turned up to tribunals like this one.

'No!' I said. 'No, no, no! No, no! Not at all. Absolutely not. But it was the Scientologists who first got me into Broadmoor. And I think one *is* coming. A man called Brian.'

'Scientologists are a funny bunch,' he said.

'They are,' I said, 'but they've been helpful to me, and haven't, you know, demanded anything weird. Just nice and helpful without wanting anything in return. I know. I'm surprised too. But what can I say?' I shrugged. 'It's the truth.'

(Actually, they had recently asked for something in return. The BBC was planning a documentary attacking them and they emailed to ask me if I'd take part in a riposte video, testifying about how helpful they'd been over the two years I'd known them. I said no. They quickly said OK, that was fine.)

Brian arrived, flustered, out of breath.

'Have I missed anything?' he asked me.

'Only a lot of mysterious busy activity,' I said. 'Something's happening but nobody will say what.'

'Hmm,' said Brian, looking around, narrowing his eyes.

And then, suddenly, a flash of colour, a maroon shirt, and some clanking. Clank clank clank.

'Oi oi!' said the guard. 'Here he comes!'

Tony looked different. His hair had been short and cropped when I'd first met him. Now it was long and quite lank. He'd put on some weight too. He was hobbling, on metal crutches.

'What happened to your leg?' Brian asked him.

'I got raspberry rippled,' said Tony. He looked around. Then he urgently whispered to Brian and me, a pleading look on his face, *'The guards beat me up.'*

'What?' I whispered back, startled.

An expression of righteous anger crossed Brian's face. His eyes darted around the ward, looking for someone to urgently take the matter up with.

'Just kidding,' Tony grinned. 'I broke it playing football.'

It was time. We entered the tribunal room. The hearing lasted all of five minutes, one of which involved the magistrates telling me that if I reported the details of what happened inside the room – who said what – I would be imprisoned. So I won't. But the upshot – Tony was to be free.

He looked like he'd been hit by a bus. Back out in the corridor his barrister, and Brian, and some independent psychiatrists he'd co-opted to his side surrounded him, congratulating him. The process would take three months – either to find him a bed for a transitional period in a medium-secure unit, or to get him straight out onto the street – but there was no doubt. He smiled, hobbled over to me, and handed me a sheaf of papers.

They were independent reports, written for the tribunal by various psychiatrists who'd been invited to assess him. They told me things I didn't know about Tony: about how his mother had been an alcoholic and used to regularly beat him up and kick him out of the house; how he'd be homeless for a few days at a time and then his mother would let him back in; how most of her boyfriends were drug addicts and criminals; how he was expelled from school for threatening his dinner lady with a knife; how he was sent to boarding and special schools but ran away because he was homesick and missed his mother.

I wondered if sometimes the difference between a psychopath in Broadmoor and a psychopath on Wall Street was the luck of being born into a stable, rich family.

Tony went off into a side room to sign some things with his solicitor. I continued looking through the papers.

Extracts from Broadmoor Case Notes

27TH SEPTEMBER 2009
    In good form.

25TH SEPTEMBER 2009
    Bright in mood.

17TH SEPTEMBER 2009
    Settled in mood and behaviour. Spent the

whole afternoon in association interacting with staff and fellow patients.

5TH SEPTEMBER 2009

Showed staff a character he'd created on the X-Box. The character was female, black-skinned and had deliberately been designed to look unattractive — almost zombie-like in facial features. He said he designed the character after a member of staff. The staff member talking to him said that was nasty and inappropriate and told him to change the name of the character several times. He refused and said she should be able to take a joke. The creation of this character would not appear to be a genuine joke but an expression of his dislike and disrespect for her.

25TH AUGUST 2009

Volley ball today. Later interacting with fellow patients and staff appropriately.

Then there were the conclusions.

OPINION

The issue is entirely dangerousness. He is not unintelligent. He has remained clean all along. If he goes out and commits a further offence he will get IPP [indeterminate sentence for public protection] with a very long tariff — there is no doubt about that whatsoever and he must be told that, which I forgot to do.

I would recommend absolute discharge. I

> think the evidence is that his mental disorder is neither of a nature or degree which makes it appropriate for him to be treated in a psychiatric hospital any longer. I do not think he needs to be detained in the interest of his health, safety, or for the protection of others. I do not consider he is dangerous.

'The thing is, Jon,' said Tony, as I looked up from the papers, 'what you've got to realize, is everyone is a bit psychopathic. You are. I am.' He paused. 'Well, obviously *I* am,' he said.

'What will you do now?' I asked.

'Maybe move to Belgium,' he said. 'There's this woman I fancy. But she's married. I'll have to get her divorced.'

'Well, you know what they say about psychopaths,' I said.

'We're *manipulative*!' said Tony.

The nurse who had cryptically told me earlier of his strong opinions about Tony came over.

'So?' I said.

'It's the right decision,' he said. 'Everyone thinks he should be out. He's a good guy. His crime was horrible, and it was right that he was locked away for a long time, but he lost years of his life to Broadmoor and he shouldn't have.'

'Does everyone feel that way?' I asked. 'Even Professor Maden?'

I looked over at him. I thought he might seem

disappointed, or even worried, but in fact he looked delighted. I wandered over.

'Ever since I went on a Bob Hare course I've believed that psychopaths are monsters,' I said, 'they're just *psychopaths*, it's what defines them, it's what they *are*.' I paused. 'But isn't Tony kind of a *semi*-psychopath? A grey area? Doesn't his story prove that people in the middle shouldn't necessarily be defined by their maddest edges?'

'I think that's right,' he replied. 'Personally I don't like the way Bob Hare talks about psychopaths almost as if they are a different species.'

Tony was standing alone now, staring at the wall.

'He does have a very high level of some psychopathic traits,' he said. 'He never takes responsibility, everything is somebody else's fault, but not of others. He's not a serious, predatory offender. So he can be a bully in the right circumstances but he doesn't set out to do serious harm for its own sake. I would also say you can never reduce any person to a diagnostic label. Tony has many endearing qualities when you look beyond the label.'

I looked over at Tony. I thought for a second that he was crying. But he wasn't. He was just standing there.

'Even if you don't accept those criticisms of Bob Hare's work,' Professor Maden was continuing, 'it's obvious if you look at his checklist you can get a high score by being impulsive and irresponsible or by coldly planning to do something. So very different people end up with the same score.' He paused. 'One needs to be careful about Tony's endearing qualities, though – many people with very damaged personalities have charisma, or some other quality that draws people in.'

'What do you think will happen to him?' I asked.

'His destiny is in his own hands,' he shrugged.

Tony's destiny, as it turned out, was not in his own hands. He was, indeed, released from Broadmoor, on 1 April 2010, but when he called me that following June he was, he said, 'out of the frying pan and into the fire. They've sent me to Bethlem, Jon, formally known as Bedlam, and they don't seem to be very keen to let me out.'

Bedlam: an institution with a history so fearsome its name is a synonym for chaos and pandemonium.

'When I say out of the frying pan and into the fire I mean it,' Tony continued. 'The other night someone actually tried to set the ward on fire.'

'How do you spend your days?' I asked him.

'I sit here doing fucking nothing,' he replied. 'Getting fat on takeaways.'

'What are your new neighbours like?' I asked. 'They can't be as intimidating as the Stockwell Strangler and the Tiptoe Through The Tulips Rapist, right?'

'They're *way* worse. There's some real head cases here.'

'Like who?'

'Tony Ferrera. Look him up. You'll find him a real piece of work. He was living in a crack house and he was out walking one day when he saw some woman. He raped her, stabbed her, set her on fire. He's here. There's Mark Gingell. Double rapist and whatnot . . .'

'Are any of them all right to hang out with?'

'No.'

'Are you scared?'

'Absolutely. If you're not scared of these people there would really be something wrong with you.'

'Oh, speaking of which,' I said, 'I've been meaning to tell you about my day with Toto Constant. He used to run a Haitian death squad. Now he's in jail for mortgage fraud. When I met him he kept saying he really wanted people to like him. He was very sensitive to people's feelings about him. I thought, "That's not very psychopathic." '

'Right,' said Tony. 'That just sounds sad.'

'So finally I said to him, "Isn't that a weakness, wanting people to like you that much?" And he said, "No it isn't! If you can get people to like you, you can manipulate them to do whatever you want them to." '

'Jesus!' Tony said. 'That's a proper psychopath.'

He paused. 'I didn't even *think* of that!' he said. 'My hand to God, that didn't even cross my *mind*.'

In early January 2011, not long after he sent me an Xmas text ('Friends are the fruit cake of life – some nutty, some soaked in alcohol, some sweet . . .') Tony was released from Bethlem.

I think the madness business is filled with people like Tony, reduced to their maddest edges. Some, like Tony, are locked up in DSPD units for scoring too high on Bob's checklist. Others are on TV at 9 p.m., their dull, ordinary, non-mad attributes skilfully edited out, benchmarks of how we shouldn't be. There are obviously a lot of very ill people out there. But there are also people in the middle, getting over-labelled, becoming nothing more than a big splurge of madness in the minds of the people who benefit from it.

Bob Hare was passing through Heathrow, and so we met one last time.

'The guy I've been visiting at Broadmoor,' I said, stirring my coffee. 'Tony. He has just been released.'

'Oh dear,' said Bob.

I looked at him.

'Well, he's gone to Bethlem,' I said. 'But I'm sure he'll be out on the streets soon.' I paused. 'His clinician was critical of you,' I said. 'He said you talked about psychopaths almost as if they were a different species.'

'All the research indicates they're not a different species,' said Bob. 'There's no evidence that they form a different species. So he's misinformed on the literature. He should be up to date on the literature. It's dimensional. He must know that. It's dimensional.'

'Obviously it's dimensional,' I said. 'Your checklist scores anything from zero to forty. But he was referring to the *general* way you talk about psychopaths . . .'

'Oh yeah,' said Bob, coldly. 'I know.'

'That's what he meant,' I said.

'It's a *convenience*,' said Bob. 'If we talk of someone with high blood pressure we talk of them as hypertensives. It's a *term*. This guy doesn't understand this particular concept. Saying "psychopathic" is like saying "hypertensive". I could say, "Someone who scores at or above a certain point on the PCL-R Checklist." That's tiresome. So I refer to them as psychopaths. And this is what I mean by psychopathy: I mean a score in the upper range of the PCL-R. I'm not sure how high it has to be. For research thirty is convenient but it's not absolute.'

Bob looked evenly at me. 'I'm in the clear on this,' he said. There was a silence. 'My gut feeling, though, deep down, is that maybe they are different,' he added. 'But we haven't established that yet.'

'I think my Broadmoor guy is a semi-psychopath,' I said.

Bob shrugged. He didn't know Tony.

'So should we define him by his psychopathy or by his sanity?' I said.

'Well, the people who say that kind of thing,' Bob said, 'and I don't use this in a pejorative way, are very left-wing, left-leaning academics. Who don't like labels. Who don't like talking about differences between people.' He paused. 'People say I define psychopathy in pejorative terms. How else can I do it? Talk about the *good* things? I could say he's a good talker. He's a good kisser. He dances very well. He has good table manners. But at the same time he screws around and kills people. So what am I going to *emphasize*?'

Bob laughed, and I laughed too.

'Ask a victim to look at the positive things and she'll say, "I can't. My eyes are swollen," ' Bob said.

Sure, Bob said, over-labelling occurs. But it's being perpetrated by the drug companies. 'Just wait and see what happens when they develop a drug for psychopathy. The threshold's going to go down, to twenty-five, twenty . . .'

'I think being a psychopath-spotter turned me a bit power-mad,' I said. 'I think I went a bit power-mad after doing your course.'

'Knowledge is power,' Bob said.

Then he shot me a pointed look. 'Why haven't *I* gone power mad, I wonder?' he said.

A few weeks later a package arrived. It was postmarked *Gothenburg, Sweden*. In the top corner someone had written, '*Today twenty-one years have passed since The Event – now it is up to us!*'

I stared at it. Then I ripped it open.

Inside was a copy of *Being or Nothingness*. I turned it over in my hands, admiring its odd, clean beauty, the holes cut out of page 13, the cryptic words and patterns and drawings, the twenty-one blank pages.

Becoming a recipient of *Being or Nothingness* was a great surprise but not an entirely unexpected one. Petter had emailed me a few days earlier to tell me I'd soon receive something in the mail, and there would be a message for me in it, and I might not understand the message immediately, but it was an important one, and I should persevere, and perhaps even consult with my peers.

'It took me eighteen years to figure out how to execute stage 1,' he wrote, 'so be patient, eventually you will figure out how to proceed. After tomorrow I will not be able to communicate with you anymore. It is unfortunate, but that is the way it has to be.'

'If I email you after tomorrow you won't respond?' I wrote back.

'You can email but I can't answer,' he replied. 'It is just the way it has to be.'

And so I had a one-day window to fire as many questions at him as I could. I began by asking him why every other page in the book was blank.

'I'm surprised that no one has commented on this before but this is of course no coincidence,' he replied. 'Twenty-one pages with text and twenty-one blank equals forty-two pages (*Being or Nothingness*). I thought it would be quite obvious.'

'All that intricate manual work – carefully cutting out the letters on page 13, and so on – did you do it alone or did you have help?'

'I do all the cut-outs, the sticker attachment, insert of "the letter to professor Hofstadter" myself,' he replied. 'A rather tedious task.'

'What about the recipients?' I emailed. 'Why were they chosen? What was the pattern?'

He didn't reply right away. I stared at the inbox. Then it came: 'There has to be a little mystery left,' he wrote.

And with that he seemed to withdraw again, as if startled by his accidental candour.

'There is nothing more I can tell you,' he wrote. 'When you receive the message, just follow your heart. As for direction, it will come to you, allow events to unfold. Now you are the chosen one, not me! You are a good person and I am sure that you will do the right thing whatever that is.'

The TV was on in the background. There was a show on about how Lindsay Lohan was 'losing it Britney-style'.

'Now you are the chosen one, not me! You are a good person and I am sure that you will do the right thing whatever that is.'

Without stopping to think I wrote him a mea culpa email, telling him that when I first met him, when I'd door-stepped him back in Gothenburg, I had dismissed him as just eccentric and obsessive. I had reduced him in that manner. But now I could see that it was his eccentricities and his obsessions that had led him to produce and distribute *Being or Nothingness* in the most intriguing ways. There is no evidence that we've been placed on this planet to be especially happy or especially normal. And in fact our unhappiness and our strangeness, our anxieties and compulsions, those least fashionable aspects of our personalities, are quite often what lead us to do rather interesting things.

He emailed me back: 'I can get a little obsessive – that I must admit . . .'

And then, as he'd promised he would, he shut off all email contact.

Now I turned the book over in my hands, and something fell out. It was an envelope, with my name written on it, and a tiny sticker of a dolphin.

Feeling unexpectedly excited, I ripped it open.

It was a card: a painting of a butterfly and a blue iris. I opened the card. And handwritten inside was the message, which comprised just two words . . .

NOTES, SOURCES, BIBLIOGRAPHY, ACKNOWLEDGEMENTS

Being my first readers can, I think, be quite a stressful experience, as I have a tendency to hand over the manuscript and then just stand there exuding a silent mix of defiance and despair. My wife, Elaine, William Fiennes, Emma Kennedy and Derek Johns and Christine Glover at AP Watt therefore deserve my biggest thanks.

There were four or five pages in the chapter 'The Night of the Living Dead' that were boring and I needed someone to tell me. Ben Goldacre was happy, maybe a little excessively happy, to do so. Adam Curtis and Rebecca Watson were brilliantly clever sounding boards as were my editors Geoff Kloske at Riverhead and Paul Baggaley at Picador, and Camilla Elworthy and Kris Doyle.

I'm very grateful to Lucy Greenwell for helping to research and set up my Gothenburg trip.

I recorded an early version of 'The Man Who Faked

Madness' for the Chicago Public Radio show *This American Life*. Thanks as always to Sarah Koenig, Ira Glass and Julie Snyder.

My research into Harry Bailey and Deep Sleep Treatment came from *Medical Murder: Disturbing Cases of Doctors who Kill* by Robert M. Caplan (Allen and Unwin, 2009).

Information about L. Ron Hubbard's life and death came from Scientology videos and from the 1997 Channel 4 documentary *Secret Lives: L. Ron Hubbard*, produced and directed by Jill Robinson and 3BM films.

I enjoyed piecing together the Elliott Barker/Oak Ridge story. Research into Dr Barker's odyssey took me to *R. D. Laing: A Life by Adrian Laing* (Sutton publishing, 1994–2006); 'Baring the Soul: Paul Bindrim, Abraham Maslow and "Nude Psychotherapy" ' by Ian Nicholson (*Journal of the History of the Behavioral Sciences*, Wiley Periodicals, Inc: Volume 43 (4) Fall 2007); and *Please Touch* by Jane Howard (McGraw-Hill, 1970).

I learnt about the Oak Ridge experiment from reading *An Evaluation of a Maximum Security Therapeutic Community for Psychopaths and Other Mentally Disordered Offenders* by Marnie E. Rice, Grant T. Harris, and Catherine A. Cormier (Plenum Publishing, 1992), 'Reflections on the Oak Ridge Experiment with Mentally Disordered Offenders, 1965–1968', by Richard Weisman (*International Journal of Law and Psychiatry*, Vol. 18, 1995), *The Total Encounter Capsule* by Elliott T. Barker M.D. and Alan J. McLaughlin (Can. Psychiatr. Assoc., 1977), and *Total Encounters: The Life and Times of the Mental Health Centre at Penetanguishene*, by Robert F. Neilson (McMaster University Press, 2000). Thanks to

Catherine Cormier and Pat Reid from Oak Ridge and to Joel Rochon.

I pieced together the Bob Hare chapter in part through my interviews with him, but also from reading his books *Without Conscience: The Disturbing World of the Psychopaths Among Us* (The Guildford Press, 1999) and *Snakes in Suits: When Psychopaths Go to Work* (Harper, 2007), which he co-authored with Paul Babiak.

The Nicole Kidman story Bob Hare tells comes from the article 'Psychopaths Among Us' by Robert Hercz, 2001.

My information on the Jack Abbott/Norman Mailer story came from 'The Strange Case of the Writer and the Criminal' by Michiko Kakutani (*New York Times Book Review*, September 20th, 1981) and *In The Belly of the Beast* by Jack Henry Abbott with an Introduction by Norman Mailer (Vintage, 1991).

Background into the crimes of Emmanuel 'Toto' Constant came from 'Giving "The Devil" His Due' by David Grann (*Atlantic*, June 2001).

Thanks to Ben Blair and Alan Hayling for their help with the chapter 'Night of the Living Dead', and to John Byrne for his book *Chainsaw: The Notorious Career of Al Dunlap in the Era of Profit at Any Price* (Harper Business, 1999) along with his research into Al Dunlap in the magazines *Business Week* and *Fast Company*.

My quest to understand the relationship between Al Dunlap's restructuring ruthlessness and Sunbeam's massive share price hike took me to Michael Shermer, Joel Dimmock, Paul Zak and Ali Arik. Thanks to them all.

Thanks to Laura Parfitt and Simon Jacobs, producers on my BBC Radio 4 series *Jon Ronson On . . .* for help with the David Shayler story and Merope Mills and Liese Spencer at *Guardian Weekend* for help with Paul Britton. The Colin Stagg/Paul Britton fiasco has been written about most interestingly in the books *The Rachel Files* by Keith Pedder (Blake Publishing, 2002), *The Jigsaw Man* by Paul Britton (Corgi Books, 1998) and *Who Really Killed Rachel?* by Colin Stagg and David Kessler (Greenzone Publishing, 1999).

Research into DSM-IV and the chapter 'The Avoidable Death of Rebecca Riley' took me to four brilliant sources – 'Dictionary of Disorder: How one man revolutionized psychiatry' by Alix Spiegel (the *New Yorker*, January 3, 2005), *The Trap* by Adam Curtis (BBC Television), 'The Encyclopedia of Insanity – A Psychiatric Handbook Lists a Madness for Everyone' by L. J. Davis (*Harpers Magazine*, February 1997) and 'Pediatric Bipolar Disorder: An object of study in the creation of an illness' by David Healy and Joanna Le Noury (North Wales Department of Psychological Medicine, Cardiff University, Bangor, 2007).

Thanks to Alistair Stevenson for giving me a beautiful line that summed up my feelings about those ideologues whose love of polemics and distrust of psychiatry blind them to the very real suffering of people with unusual mental-health symptoms.

'Let me state for the record: at his best, Ronson is one of the finest comic writers working today. I began *The Psychopath Test* late at night, tired, dispirited and ill – then found myself laughing like the proverbial loon for page after page. It's all about timing, of course: by inserting his own character with a forensic skill into the very real and frightening world that surrounds us all, Ronson achieves a gag rate that puts him on a par with that master nebech Woody Allen . . . By constructing his books so that they start off achingly funny then at a certain juncture become naggingly painful, [Ronson] does indeed force us to think more deeply about the subject at hand'
Will Self, *Guardian*

'Ronson has a fine journalist's nose for sniffing out the most entertaining monsters to interview . . . *The Psychopath Test* is a sort of patchwork of stories about madness, and the variety of ways in which it is diagnosed. It is full of strange characters, ranging from the slightly nutty to the stark raving bonkers . . . Ronson is such a chirpy, inquisitive and funny writer'
Craig Brown, *Mail on Sunday*

'[An] entertaining exploration of madness . . . What is clear from this fun account is that anyone who is in a position to use a test for psychopaths needs to treat it with care. One misunderstood personality trait and the wrong man could end up in Broadmoor. Or on the board of a FTSE 100 company. Both outcomes are pretty terrifying'
Sunday Times

'Ronson's self-deprecating tone makes him the ideal man to explore the uncertain world of insanity ... A thoughtful and funny read, this book's guaranteed to leave you a little unsettled'   'Book of the Week' *Stylist*

'For seasoned Ronson-watchers, this is a typical treat, a semi-sinister, half-hilarious trip into the dark side, as he stumbles around, upsetting his subjects with a mix of probing investigation and social faux-pas'   *List*

'As if his Loony Tunes run-ins with men who stare at goats were not bad or mad enough, Ronson is now way-laid by a code-cracking quest that leads him to suspect that there is madness everywhere and that society is not based on rationality but built on insanity ... Like Louis Theroux or the good cop, Ronson acts the straight man or Mr Nice Guy. With disarming irony, he flips the coin of the perceived world to turn it to its disturbing obverse'
The Times

'Both screamingly funny and deeply disturbing ... Jon Ronson has carved out a niche as a witty chronicler of the eccentric and deluded, so he is perfectly suited to document the foibles of the insanity industry ... Many of the interviews are the stuff of black comedy ... Ronson's still, small voice of reason triumphs in the end, and he has produced a thought-provoking, wry, incisive book that challenges the cherished orthodoxies at the heart of the psychiatric profession'

Tatler, Book of the Month

PHOTO CREDITS

Not
The End